INTO HIS SPLENDID LIGHT

AMERICAN BENEDICTINE ACADEMY STUDIES ·

Into
His Splendid Light

BY ALBAN BOULTWOOD, O.S.B.
Abbot of St. Anselm's Abbey

WITH A FOREWORD BY
Eugene J. McCarthy, United States Senate

SHEED AND WARD · NEW YORK

© Sheed and Ward, Inc., 1968

Library of Congress Catalog Card Number: 68-13843

Nihil obstat: Kevin Seasoltz, O.S.B., Censor, English Cong.
of St. Benedict; Imprimi potest: Victor Farwell, O.S.B.,
Abbot President; Nihil obstat: Bernard Theall, O.S.B., Censor deputatus; Imprimatur: ✠Patrick Cardinal O'Boyle,
Archbishop of Washington, July 6, 1967. The nihil obstat
and imprimatur are official declarations that a book or
pamphlet is free of doctrinal or moral error. No implica-
tion is contained therein that those who have granted the
nihil obstat and the imprimatur agree with the content,
opinions or statements expressed.

Excerpts from The Constitutions, Decrees, and Declarations of the Ecumenical Council are taken from The
Documents of Vatican II, published by Guild Press,
America Press, Association Press, and Herder and Herder,
and copyrighted 1966 by The America Press. Used by
permission.

Manufactured in the United States of America

| Contents

Contents

| Foreword

Abbot Boultwood's meditations place individual and personal piety or spirituality in the context, first, of community, and then, in the context of growth and change.

He offers no new techniques or shortcuts to perfection, nor does he claim to have discovered new texts or offer surprising new interpretations or applications of the old. The Benedictine way has never been the way of sudden conversion, but of continuing effort in combining work and prayer without sharp distinction between the secular and the spiritual.

"One of the most special graces of this life is time itself," writes Abbot Boultwood in one of his meditations, "time for repentance, time for growth, time for perseverance, time for change, and—most of all—time for beginning again."

Abbot Boultwood does not attempt to write the last act in the play of salvation, but to give directives and helps as we move through the complexities and confusions of the second act of life, and of history, both temporal and redemptive.

EUGENE J. MCCARTHY

| Introduction

One of the great rediscoveries of the Second Vatican Council was the dignity, freedom, and responsibility of the individual human person. Together with this came renewed emphasis on the universal vocation to holiness: "All the faithful of Christ of whatever rank or status are called to the fullness of the Christian life and to the perfection of charity" (Dogmatic Constitution on the Church, Par. 40). The whole purpose of this great pastoral Council might be expressed in apostolic words: "Our message concerns that Word, who is life . . . this message we pass on to you, so that you too may share in our fellowship. What is this fellowship of ours? Fellowship with the Father, and with his Son Jesus Christ . . . See what love the Father has given us, that we should be called children of God, and so we are" (cf. I John 1:1-4; 3:1).

All our preoccupation with the Church in its institutional aspects must not blind us to the fact that it is not finally as an institution that the Church of Christ lives in this world of men and their concerns. The Church is not a rival organization competing with the proper institutions of human society: "My kingdom is not of this world." The Church lives in the world and enters into its affairs insofar as she lives in individual men and in their actions. She offers the truth of Christ by which men must form their consciences, and the grace of his Spirit to help them make their choices and thus build their society. She should be visible and effectual among men, therefore, not primarily as an institution, but as a vital presence in the personal lives of her children. It lies in their power either to manifest or to conceal. All of the faithful are incorporated by baptism into Christ and share his redemptive mission in the world, whatever be their special vocation in life: the priesthood, the religious life, the lay state. Each state of life bears witness in its own special way. Priests proclaim the gospel, fulfilling the Lord's command: "Go into the whole world and preach the gospel to every creature." Religious offer their witness by living and working in the spirit of the evangelical counsels. The laity have the great and difficult vocation of living in the full reality and stress of temporal affairs, and yet standing before the world in witness to the resurrection and life of the Lord Jesus as a sign that God lives. The Council Fathers do not hesitate to see this as a divine vocation: "They are called there by God so that . . . being led by the spirit of the gospel they can work for the sanctification of the world from within" (Dogmatic Constitution on the Church, Par. 31).

The reflections in this book are offered in the humble hope that they may be of some service to all men and women following their Christian vocation. They are offered by one who is well aware that in a monastery he misses many of the trials, and also many of the opportunities, of the ordinary circumstances of family, social, and apostolic life. But over the years he has learned with affection and admiration how willingly and gratefully men and women look to the monasteries as to "schools of the Lord's service" (St. Benedict's own phrase), where they may find guidance and encouragement in their Christian life, "being led by the spirit of the gospel." For there is really only one great vocation which we all share, bishops, monks, layfolk, only one that matters, only one that is eternal: to love God with our whole heart and our whole soul and our whole strength; to be called and to be children of God. This is the one divine vocation to which we are all called in Christ; all the other "vocations" are but means to fulfill this one. It is not at all strange, then, that some words from St. Benedict's prologue to his Rule, citing also Psalm 33, apply very aptly for our present purpose: "God says to you 'If you will have true and everlasting life turn away from evil and do good; seek peace and pursue it . . . my eyes shall be upon you and my ears open to your prayers; and before you call upon me I will say to you, Behold, I am here.' In faith and good works then, let us walk in his paths by the guidance of the gospel." It is in this spirit, and in the joyful confidence that even before we turn to our Father he has turned to us, that I offer the following reflections on the paschal mystery of Christian life, death, and resurrection, in Christ and in us his brothers and sisters.

But you are a chosen race, a royal priesthood, a consecrated nation, a people set apart to sing the praises of God who called you out of the darkness into his splendid light.

—1 Peter 2:9

INTO HIS SPLENDID LIGHT

Advent

1 | Beginning of the Beginning

One of the most special graces of this life is time itself. There is time for repentance, time for growth, time for perseverance, time for change, and—most of all—time for beginning again. If only we recognized our providential situation in this world, we should always be saying, "Thank God, I do have time: time for salvation, time for grace." As one year comes to an end, another year of the Lord begins, another year of grace, another time for response to Christ's always timely, always newly working Holy Spirit.

This grace of new life and ever new beginning is a constant and characteristic feature of Christian life on this earth. The Spirit is always crying out to us, through the voice of the Church, through holy scripture, to be renewed, to walk in newness of life, to put on the new man, to put on Christ—Christ who is ever ancient, ever new; Christ yesterday, today, the same forever. This is the Christian vocation until the end of time itself, when all things will be made new in Christ, when God is all in all. Every soul is to be saved and sanctified and made new in Christ; and somehow, too, very beautifully, all are to be gathered into that new and perfect unity which is Christ's body, the new Jerusalem.

But it seems that besides this deep unceasing work of renewal for mankind's salvation, there are special and more crucial times of renewal, when grace is offered in an extraordinary way, when the need is more urgent, the summons clearer. And it is certain that we live in such a time.

Some of you may remember that at one point in the Second World War, when at last the tide of the conflict seemed to be turning, Winston Churchill expressed our hope strikingly: "We must not speak of it as the beginning of the end; but perhaps it is the end of the beginning." And now, in these first years after the Second Vatican Council, we are only at the beginning of the beginning. It is really not much more than that at present, not much more than great documents promulgated but not yet producing their effect. It is still mainly just words, not reality. But the words are great words and bear the seed of new life, and already we feel the Spirit stirring in the Church and in the world, promising new life, new growth.

In some ways it is a solemn and uncomfortable prospect. Change always has some aspects unwelcome to our nature; we feel disturbed, insecure. But, more important, it means a special responsibility for our generation, a special readiness in mind and heart, in faith and obedience and love, to respond to the movement of the Spirit in our time. Let us pray and strive to be ready. For it is a clear and painful, and sometimes shameful, lesson of history that unless the Church of God is renewed and reformed from within, in head and members, it must suffer a kind of violent reformation from without, at the price of defection, heresy, and schism. Furthermore, without wishing to sound too pessimistic or sensational, we cannot help being aware of the heavy threat of thermonuclear ordeal that hangs over our generation; and we uncomfortably realize that there could be one very sudden and violent way of reformation, with some small remnant of mankind and of the Church beginning only too truly anew.

The full teaching authority of the Church of Christ, formally assembled in General Council, has most solemnly summoned us all to renewal. Sixteen great documents have been promulgated—on the Church herself, her worship, her priesthood, her people, her religious, her missions, her education, her freedom, her relations with the whole world. All are concerned with reform and renewal, with new understanding, new spirit, new reality, new hope, new beginnings. And the great essential practical point is that *we* are the Church; there can be no renewal, no reform in the Church, unless there is renewal and reform in us.

All this self-study, new thinking, and new attitude in the Church is not a weakening of faith. On the contrary, it is a striving for a deeper, more explicit, more deliberate, and more conscious faith, for a more truly personal and human response to the grace of supernatural faith. It would be a total misunderstanding of the whole purpose of *aggiornamento* to see it merely as an attempt to make the Catholic Church more acceptable to—and, as it were, more at home in—this world. It is a most earnest (almost desperate, because almost too late) attempt to summon the full force of Christ's truth and love to meet the urgent questions and realities of the men and women of this age. It is the Church's great attempt to know and help and redeem our time, our world, through her faithful witness to the true eternal values.

For this, our hope and our faith rest always in our Lord Jesus Christ and his promise, his promise to be with us all days and to send his Spirit to teach us his truth. But God always deals with us in a living way, not mechanically, but creatively, worthily. So his teaching means our learning, his truth our sincerity, his giving our receiving, his acting our reacting. And he comes not once and for all, in merely historical record; he comes *all* days; his is a living, active presence. He comes in different ways at different times, according to the need of each day, according to the readiness and willingness of each generation. And, likewise, our own personal faith, our own commitment to Christ, is not really just made once and for all, not something we are merely legally enrolled in. It is something we make new each day, make true each day. In each day, with all its burdens and choices, we find the real material of our commitment to Christ, our response to his coming, our faith in his Spirit. Each dying daily is a daily living in Christ.

After all, what we are really concerned with in all our renewal is not a question of liturgical laws, or ecclesiology, or canon law, or apologetics, but the supreme and vital mystery of God's redemptive presence in our humanity: how the mystery and tragedy of human life are enlightened and given meaning and hope in Jesus Christ. Therefore, by all means let us study and talk and think about our faith, our Church, her teaching, especially in the great documents of Vatican II. We must not let it be too long before the Church which has been given the Second Vatican Council truly is the Church of the Council. A beginning must be made. But, at the same time, we must give ourselves, with faith stronger than ever, with courage, peace, and hope, to the great positive optimistic revelation of the Spirit of God in his Church, to the gift of divine life, to our vocation to holiness, to the fulfillment in us of the eternal purpose. "This is the will of God, your sanctification."

2 | A New Song

Holy scripture constantly encourages us to "sing to the Lord a new song." There is deep meaning in this, and there are many ways in which we may fulfill it. We always owe our song of worship and love to God; and it is ever a new song, for God is the God of newness. He is the God of life, of the living waters which spring ever fresh from his creative mind and heart; he is the source and ground of all being, of beauty ever ancient and ever new.

But beyond all other manifestations of the divine newness, and beyond all other new songs in the heart of humanity for its God, is the surpassing canticle of the Incarnation. The new birth of the Son of God in our flesh is the wholly new song of love, the transcendent hymn of God's redemptive love for his creatures. Now at last, in the heart of Christ, comes the perfect response of mankind in newness of life and love. This wholly new revelation of God's love, not merely announced to us but actually embodied in our flesh by the incarnation of the eternal Word, is the new canticle which now we sing forever to the Lord.

We speak of the present age of the Church as an age of renewal. This is true; but all renewal must draw its life and soul from that supreme renewal begun when the Son of God entered into our world to restore all things to his Father, to bring all things back to the sublime Beginning. At Christmas

9

we shall pray "that your only Son's new birth in the flesh may free us from our old slavery to sin." This is the new covenant, the new promise of God to man, the new divine communication of that which we call the life of grace, of faith. This is the beginning of the redemptive renewal which will only be completed when God comes at the dawn of all, saying, "Behold, I make all things new."

We are always really starting anew in our Christian life. No matter what may have been the failures and weariness of the "old man," it only takes one act of new sorrow, of new faith, of new hope, of new love, and all the past is finished with—a new life begins. At that moment, at every moment, even at the last moment of our mortality, God is the God of newness of life. This is his divine prerogative. All our "oldness" is transformed by his renewing love: "Send forth your Spirit and they shall be created; and you will renew the face of the earth."

At every level of creation this process is going on without ceasing. There is a constant alternation in being, an unfailing growth of new from old. This holds true from the slow relentless processes of the grinding strata of the rocks of the earth, through the dazzling fluctuations of light in the galaxies of stars, to the even deeper and swifter processes of the human spirit. And, by the supernatural gift of God's grace, there is the constant merciful renewal of our soul in a wholly new kind of existence. By baptism and faith we are new creatures, a new creation far more sublime than our natural birth. And we know that baptism is not a "thing" received once in our life, but a continuing communication, a link with the creative Godhead, renewing and enlivening our soul day by day, until our journey is done and we enter into the presence of that Lord for whom baptism's water and chrism first washed and anointed us.

The deep instincts of our humanity are reflected in many different aspects of our nature, some good and innocent, some amusing, some perverted and evil. Newness certainly exercises a strong attraction over us in many ways. We cannot walk through a store without seeing the word NEW glaring at us in blazing colors from every package on every shelf. It seems that to sell at all, a thing has to be "new." Indeed, the industrial psychologists could hardly have missed this one; for we recognize this very clearly in ourselves. We all like new clothes, new sights, new books. I have even heard it suggested that the great attraction of the game of golf is that each hole is a new beginning. As one tees off for the ninth hole, all the blunders and catastrophies of the eighth are left behind. And even in matters in which newness might be a little suspect, as in friendship or thought, there is no denying that we are attracted disproportionately by new friends and new ideas. It is an attraction which does not always survive the test of time. In fact, this is one of the dangers of our own "age of renewal"; it is so easy at times to be captivated by mere novelty. The element of newness on this earth, like everything else, has its own imperfections and dangers— which the glorious eternal newness of heaven will never know. Yet, as usual, God draws good out of the limitations of his creatures. There is a special grace and virtue to be gained in our patient journeying and struggling with time and change, with old and new. There is a special mercy in the fact that we *can* change, that we can turn from the old evil to the new good, that we can turn from sin and find forgiveness, that we can at any moment find newness of life.

This is really the wonderful message of Advent, as once more the great cycle of grace begins to turn, once more the joyful canticle of redemption is announced. The angels of the Nativity sing their heavenly heraldry: "Behold, I bring you good news of great rejoicing for the whole people." It is the good news of the Incarnation, of salvation for the world; old things pass away, all things become new. Time and time again, in infinite mercy, this great new Word is announced in our old world. It ought to have been heard at once, in wonder and joy and thanks. But such is our weakness and waywardness and forgetfulness that "his own received him not." Yet God takes pity on his creation, so darkened and perplexed by sin; and through his Church he announces year after year, until the end of time, the coming of his Son in grace and redemption, in humility and patience and love, asking to be received, until that last day of Coming, when he will call all creation into the presence of the Father, and there will be a new heaven and new earth—"for behold, I make all things new."

Meanwhile, this renewal must go on according to the reality of our own personal human life, in spirit and in truth: by our willing, sincere, persevering cooperation, using all the faculties of our body and soul, of our mind and heart. To help us respond appropriately during these weeks before Christmas, the Advent liturgy leads us far back into the "oldness," into the Old Testament, into the long centuries of waiting for the Savior. In this way we are helped to realize our great need of the Redeemer; to acknowledge our guilt, our weakness, our danger; to pray, to yearn, to prepare, and above all to hope. Our hope springs up afresh, as the Savior comes in new grace; our hope is strengthened, as we realize that God cares so much about "his failures." (These are, of course, *our* failures; but he makes them *his own*.) So many of our Lord's parables illustrate his care about the weak one, the missing one, the sinner. The ninety-nine sheep are left while the stray one is sought; there is disproportionate (it would seem) rejoicing over the little coin that is found; and, perhaps most strikingly, there is the moving story of the prodigal son. All our faith teaches us that the whole redemptive love of God is now sent forth in the incarnate Savior to seek us, to save us from failure, to bring us new life. So we pray: "Come Lord, do not delay." "Drop down dew you heavens"; may our poor weary souls be refreshed and renewed in the Just One.

3 | The Traveler

We are preparing for the advent of a traveler, for the coming of him who was sent from his own heavenly home to our far country, so distant and lost in its sinfulness. And during Christ's sojourn upon our earth, he was always a traveler, always on his way to his goal. In one terrible way that goal might always be seen as Calvary. It was that, but it was more than that. His only goal, his constant unfaltering purpose, was always his Father's will—that is, his loving fulfillment of his Father's will for our salvation.

That is really our goal too, the Father's will, our salvation. And in Christ the first great essential step has already been taken, the great price paid. But this has to be true in us also, and the work of salvation must go on until the end of time, as long as there is a single soul to be saved. So we too follow Christ, seeking to fulfill his Father's will, laboriously and falteringly, but knowing that the achievement will be perfect and glorious in the heavenly home to which we are traveling.

If we could keep more clearly in mind the great fact that we are really travelers in this world, we should not feel so disappointed and frustrated by the ordinary events of our life. These disappointments are due to the very strong and perhaps very pardonable instinct in us which drives us to look for success, for achievement in all sorts of ways: social, business, professional, and even (in not quite the right way) spiritual. This is really a characteristic instinct of this world. We want to feel that we have attained something, some degree of success, of fulfillment; or, at any rate, we want to feel that we are going to achieve something. We all have a touch of Mr. Micawber's pathetic conviction that "something will turn up."

But isn't this precisely what travelers must never really look for? They cannot stop to build, to acquire, to establish themselves, to do all the things they would like to do. They must always be moving on, leaving things behind for the sake of their goal. All their achievement, all their success, all the fulfillment of their gifts and powers, will only come when they reach their journey's end. This is not to say that all the things of this world do not matter. Of course they do, but as means, as something we do along the way, not as final goals, not as something to turn us from the end. The Christian goal is always drawing us on and away, always pulling at us to resist the natural instinct to settle down, to make ourselves "at home" in this world; for we have here no abiding city.

"Come, follow me." It is a loving invitation, but a difficult one for us to accept. God himself has to help us to respond to it. So he does not leave us too much peace and success here, but drives us on by all kinds of expedients. These are really all resources of a most providential and loving kindness. Because of our disordered instincts and appetites, however, they require sacrifice and cause us pain; but they call us to wrench ourselves away from many things that would delay us on our journey.

Christ came to bring truth into this world, not simply intellectual knowledge, but essential truth: truth of heart and soul, truth of right and wrong, truth of love, truth of God.

This divine traveler came to be the way, the truth, the life. It takes courage and humility for a follower of Christ to travel that same way through this world, to live so that his life shows forth truth rather than worldly wisdom. But that is exactly our vocation. Christ came to call men into his kingdom of truth and life, of holiness and grace, of justice, love, and peace. And if the way by which men follow him leads in some little degree up the hill of Calvary, that is not really his choice for us, but the choice of the enemies of truth.

Notice that our Savior did not say that he *shows* us the way, the truth, and the life; he said, "I *am* the way, the truth, and the life." The union is much closer, the communication much deeper. He comes to be himself the bridge over the terrible gulf, to be himself the strength for our weakness in this journey. So he comes first to share what is ours—indeed, to share what we are—and then to share with us what is his, what *he is!* The first step is taken for the sake of the second, that is, that the second may be taken in spirit and in truth. For our sharing in him is not to be a mere outward association, a mere legal title, but an interior reality; it is to be a true communication given not only according to God's nature of infinite goodness and love but also according to our nature. That is, it is to be received by us in truth of mind and freedom of will.

Therefore, first he has to come to us; he has to win us to himself before he can truly share himself with us. When St. John Baptist de la Salle founded his teaching Brothers of the Christian Schools, he made a strict rule that they should not become priests and should not study Latin. This seems strange until one understands that his apostolate to the poor and oppressed people of his age would have been hindered by the then almost total and hopeless gulf between the poor and the upper classes. A classical education, and even the priest-hood itself, was at that time the typical class prerogative and distinction of the rich. In order to reach the poor, the Broth-ers renounced the privileges of clergy and education, making themselves one with the poor and humble that they might truly begin to raise them up. So it was with our Savior. In the words of St. Paul: "His nature is, from the first, divine, and yet he did not see, in the rank of Godhead, a prize to be coveted; he dispossessed himself, and took the nature of a slave, fashioned in the likeness of men, and presenting him-self to us in human form."

By making himself one with us, he draws and unites us to himself; and thus he is able to communicate to us that new-ness of life, the fullness of grace and holiness of his resurrec-tion. It is for this that he comes in all the poverty and lowli-ness and humanity of Christmas: that he may make us able and worthy to share in all the riches of his divinity. He comes as a traveler, that he may draw us after him and lead us home. The message of him who was even born in a wayside stable, on a journey, is that here we are all pilgrims and travelers, that we have here no abiding city, but that we have a heav-enly city which is our true journey's end. Again as expressed by St. Paul: "So he came, and his message was of peace for you who were far off, peace for those who were near; far off or near, united in the same Spirit, we have access through him to the Father. You are no longer exiles, then, or aliens; the saints are your fellow-citizens, you belong to God's household."

That is why, through all the poignant story of suffering and traveling that begins in the poor cave at Bethlehem, we can still say: A joyful, happy Christmas!

4 | The Great Choice

The eternal God, Lord of life and Lord of history, comes into time, in meekness and humanity, offering himself to our hearts, offering himself to our free choice—the choice of acceptance or rejection. Historically, that choice has already been made; and, strangely and terribly, both alternatives have been chosen. The response of love and grace and acceptance was made when Mary said, "Let it be unto me according to your word"; the response of unbelief and loveless selfishness and rejection was made by all those of whom the Evangelist wrote, "His own received him not." In our own lives, however, this tremendous choice still confronts us all. Every human being has to face this awful alternative, to make the crucial choice before the time of choosing is ended. All the loving goodness of God's providential care is exerted to draw us to the choice of the true and the holy; all the power of darkness and deceit conspires to draw us to the false choice to which our poor fallen nature is now so liable. Which is to be our life's choice?

All the events of our life are meant to be seen in the light of this choice; and if sometimes the forces of passion and ambition impel us dangerously toward the false alternative, yet there are also seasons of special grace when the light of eternal truth and the attraction of divine goodness draw us savingly toward the Way, the Truth, and the Life.

The ending of the old year and the opening of a new year of the Lord are both seasons of grace. A deep sense of our mortality and of the nearness of eternal life urges our choice of the true and holy, our conversion from the false light of this world. Besides our constant remembrance during November of all the holy souls who have gone before us into the presence of God, there is almost always, as the years go by, someone very dear and close to us who has just taken that great clear step into eternity. For them, for our beloved dead, the great choice is made at last—made now in clarity, joy, certainty, with no fear of loss or change. "You are my God . . . to you my whole heart goes out." All the confusions and problems and weaknesses are now fallen away forever. Only God, only life, remains.

We always knew, by God's own merciful grace of faith, that there was really only one ultimate choice for us: the living God, for whom our heart is made. And in a way we have "always" made that choice; at least, we never really renounced it in principle. In practice, however, that choice is not really a once-and-for-all thing; it is never, in this life, something "done," fixed, made. It is always something making, doing; it is creative; it is living. For it is the reflection of God's own eternal choice and will. And that is not, as we rather unfortunately tend to express it, simply an eternal decree, something fixed, remote, lifeless, graven on tables of stone. God's will is life, is love, is creative, is ever new. In terms of abstract philosophy, it is doubtless correct to define God's will in terms of his own perfect and immutable nature, free from all shadow of change and alteration in weakness or imperfection. But in terms of our own human experience and psychology, it is probably more helpful to conceive of God's will as *we* know life: flexible, moving, reacting, accept-

ing, and giving. It is never a "dead letter"; it is never defeated or lost; it is always close to us, always a living and life-
giving word, even when we have turned from it in sin: "Here
is what you must do now . . ."

Similarly, our own will for God, our choice of God, is
always a living, vital, growing thing. For us this must mean,
in this life, that it is also a thing of pain, of growing pains. It
does not yet mean the fullness of perfect possession and union
that it will know in the heavenly vision. It means decisions,
choices, perplexities, even mistakes and sorrowful renunciations. But in all this and through all this our choice is something true, something sublime, for it is our will for God, our
will to accept his divine love.

All these difficulties and failures about the choice are only
there because of the dark confusion left by sin in our nature.
How deep that wound is, how disordered now our instincts
and passions, and how mortal the character of the turning
from God which was the origin of all this is clearly shown
from the very difficulty we now find in making our choice.
For what is this choice but the choice of utter goodness, perfect beauty, perfect joy? It is the choice of what our very
being is created for, yearns for, cannot rest without. We are
not confronted with some grim dilemma, some fearful risk on
either side. It is the living God who awaits our choice; it is
Love, it is Goodness, it is Life.

Yet it remains so hard and uncertain for us sometimes,
even after some glimpse of the truth and joy, so hurt and
weakened is our nature in all its powers. That Goodness, that
Love, that God, seems so remote, so hidden. So the living
God, the eternal God, came to us incarnate, in our own humanity, in our own flesh and blood. He came to be seen and
heard, to be touched and known and loved, to be accepted, to

be chosen. And now once more, at this Advent, we are offered the grace and the choice: "To you have I lifted up my soul . . . to you my whole heart goes out." A new year of the Lord repeats and continues the whole merciful round of his grace. Again comes the divine proposal of love to mankind. Again the Lord comes to consecrate our world, to draw us to himself, to be made flesh in our own hearts and souls by his life of grace in us, to be our Choice. As the old year ends, we raise our eyes in faith and hope and love once more to him who is ever new: "It is to heaven that we look expectantly for the coming of our Lord Jesus Christ to save us; he will form this humbled body of ours anew, molding it into the image of his glorified body, so effective is his power to make all things obey him."

Christmas

Christmas

5 | The Easy Mystery

The mystery of the incarnation of the Son of God is not only the most basic doctrine of our faith but also, in a slightly different sense, the most "mysterious." That the transcendent, infinite God should not only create our nature but should then unite it substantially to himself by entering into his own creation as one of our race, true man, true human—this "flesh and blood" cannot reveal to us, but only the supernatural revelation of our heavenly Father himself.

Yet, strangely, while this tremendous truth is most difficult, almost repugnant, to the human mind, especially if that mind stands proudly on its own standards of reasonableness, it has always in fact proved easy for the human heart. It is a revelation which humanity has accepted most willingly, most lovingly, with surprising ease—almost too easily—through the centuries. It is the loveliest and most attractive truth of our faith. From the simplicity of childhood, through the complexities and rebellions of youth, through the trials and perplexities of adult years, most of us by God's grace cling without difficulty, without question, to the joyful truth of the incarnation of the Son of God. It is some instinct in us, some divine instinct in us, deeper and wiser than the cold light of human reason, some supernatural sense, some touch of divine wisdom itself. It is a grateful movement of the soul by which we respond to this turning of our God toward us.

For what we are concerned with in the incarnation of our

Lord Jesus Christ is a movement of divine love. Love moves not mainly in reason or logic or philosophy; love concerns the whole living being, the deep spirit, and surpasses all words or argument or reason. Nevertheless, in order to be fulfilled and true, it does have to be manifested in some way. Love which is concealed and unknown has a certain sad frustration about it, a pity and loss. Even our human hearts know this. Love seeks to manifest and to complete itself in some way proportionate to its nature and character; it seeks to be known and returned.

Although we cannot submit divine mystery, especially the mystery of divine love, to human argument and reasoning, there are some inadequate but not altogether untrue analogies that we can apply to divine things. If even created love, at its purest and noblest, demands some noble and beautiful manifestation, then what of uncreated love? What manifestation can be proportionate and fitting for its infinite depth and beauty and goodness? Can we not answer: the incarnation of the Son of God?

Not that the incarnation of the eternal Word remains anything but a freely chosen act of infinite magnanimity and condescension. It was the *free* sign and effect of that same freely given love. But we can see, in a way, that the otherwise inexplicable, incredible fact that God became man now appears as a divinely proportionate sign of infinite love. It does remain an overwhelming mystery of divine condescension, pity, love; but it is now seen as a *credible* mystery, because this infinite gesture of incarnation is believed as the effect of infinite love. "God so loved the world as to give his only begotten Son." We give our loving grateful faith to that, and all else follows. Without the grace of faith in divine love, all else in Christian teaching is beyond belief.

And we may even make bold to say that nothing else *but* the Incarnation could really have convinced the heart of man of God's infinite, personal love. Man may come by his reason to the knowledge of God's existence, his power and wisdom, his goodness. But how, in actual human fact, could we ever have known *how* God loves us, cares for us, seeks us—unless his own Son had come to us, taken our humanity upon himself, made visible and tangible and sensible to our hearts his personal love and care for us?

All our faith, our hope, our Christian life and love, begin with the lovely feast of the human birth of the Son of God at Christmas. However worldly and indifferent mankind has become through the centuries, yet, almost in spite of itself, it returns with hope and good will to the birth of the Savior. At Christmas our faith pierces through to the heart of the Blessed Trinity, to the Source of all our life and hope and holiness. We go back to the divine Beginning, and we begin again in hope and love.

As the life of this divine child unfolds on earth, through the year to come, other mysteries will present themselves to us: the mystery of sin and our fallen nature, the mystery of redemption and newness of life. And our faith will fulfill itself in many ways: through tribulation and repentance, through perseverance and hope, through suffering and sharing in the mysterious oblation of Christ's own loving sacrifice. All that is to come, and we shall try to accept it as we adore and follow. But at Christmas we know only joy and peace and hope, and the tender beauty of the birth of Divine Love Incarnate, of him who came to show us the way, to *be* for us the Way, the Truth, the Life.

6 | He Shall Be Called Wonderful

As we meditate on the incarnation of the Son of God, there comes to mind a paradoxical but profound remark of Father Gerald Vann: "The surprising thing is, not that Jesus Christ was God, but that God was Jesus Christ." By the grace of God's own Spirit now communicated to us in the gift of faith and the light of revelation, we recognize—we can almost say easily, clearly, joyfully—the Godhead shining in Jesus Christ. We are not now surprised, perhaps not as surprised as we should be, to know that Jesus Christ was God. Every word of his, every act, every reaction, reflected the divine nature within him. Even after two thousand years, at all this distance in time, in culture, even indirectly through the written word, through sign and sacrament, through his Church, we cannot fail to recognize the eternal Son of God, the true person of Jesus Christ, true man and yet so truly God.

How much easier it is for us to recognize the truth this way—from Christ to God, from the visible to the invisible—rather than from theory or speculation about the possibility of God becoming man. Who could ever have presumed for one moment to entertain such a strange and seemingly insane and blasphemous idea: the Creator entering into his creation, the transcendent Godhead uniting himself with a man. I think such an idea had never clearly entered into the human mind, even among the chosen people of God in the Old Testament, before it actually came about. Looking back, we can indeed now recognize the distant lightning flashes of revelation in the Old Testament, heralding the One who was to come; but the New Testament itself records how imperfectly understood were these promises: "Long ago God spoke in incomplete and varied ways to our fathers through the prophets: in these, the last days, he has spoken to us through his Son, whom he has made the heir of all things, and through whom he created the ages. He is the refulgence of the Father's glory, and the very representation of his being, and he sustains all things by his powerful word." It is only in the light and presence of Jesus Christ himself that we can really come to the divine truth: he is God; and God is Jesus Christ. This wholly new and wonderful thing has come about in Christ: "A light shall shine upon us this day, for the Lord is born to us; and he shall be called WONDERFUL, God, Prince of peace, Father of the world to come."

And how wonderful Christ is! We are struck with wonder when something is *new,* a new thought, a new experience. How *new* Christ is! He brought a new beginning to our poor race, new holiness, new hope, new love: "A new commandment I give you, that you love one another." It was not exactly a new commandment; love had always been the true fulfillment of the law. But mankind had so badly forgotten and perverted it that a new revelation was needed in order that men should begin to understand again the nature of God, the nature of man, the nature of love. This new revelation came with the birth of the Son of God himself into our world.

We are filled with wonder when we find something *admirable,* something beautiful, lovely. How *admirable* Christ is! Even men who have not managed to believe in his God-

head have always found him admirable, supreme among
men, in the beauty of his person, his teaching, his life. When
he walked the roads of our earth, men were pierced by the
wonder of his person, drawn by the divine beauty that radi-
ated through his humanity: "They left all, and followed
him." We, too, feel this divine attraction: "Draw us after
Thee . . ."

We are moved with wonder in the presence of *mystery*.
And, with all his bright radiance and clarity, how *mysterious*
Christ is, how *divine!* It is that ever-present saving mystery of
Christ's divinity that enlightens every man coming into this
world. In his light, we see the light. It is indeed an overwhelming thought that God should become man; but somehow, when we know Jesus Christ, we find faith; for, in a
beautiful way, we feel in our hearts that it is *not* surprising
that Jesus Christ was God. And in his grace we easily and
joyfully proclaim our faith: "I believe in one Lord Jesus
Christ, the only-begotten Son of God, born of the Father
before all ages, God of God, light of light, true God of true
God . . . Who for us men and for our salvation came down
from heaven."

The incarnation of Christ is the beginning of our own
renewal, of our own merciful restoration to that blessed
image of God in which he created us, to be the reflection of
his goodness and truth and love. The natural reflection of
himself which the Creator first imparted to us was spoiled
and lost when man turned away from God to sin. And, ever
since, our human nature has reflected instead something of
the evil and ugliness and falsehood of sin. But, by the infinite
mercy of God, his own Son came to restore our human nature
by taking it to himself, communicating to it his own love and
truth. He came to give us back what we had lost: a sense of

the divine, a reflection and share of goodness, a response of love. True, the effects of sin do linger and trouble this world; but since Christ's birth, even where sin abounds, grace abounds still more. Christ offers the light of his truth to our minds, by faith; the warmth of his loving kindness to our hearts, by charity—so that we may know him and love him, and love as he loves.

That is why, in the true spirit of the incarnation of Christ, we open our hearts in friendship and love at Christmas. That is why our own love must truly reflect God's love, that is, God's gift of love, a love freely poured out, excluding none, seeking all. So Christmas means not only the sweet welcome joy of turning to our friends, but also the more arduous, deeper love which turns to those we cannot yet call our friends, especially to these last, for this is truly the divine spirit of Christ's incarnation. Christ came to us when we were yet strangers and sinners; it was because he first loved us that he saved us and sanctified us, gathered us into his household, restored his likeness in us. So now we must first give love to those who seem to be our enemies, who do not yet return our friendship, those who mistrust and even hate us. These, too, we must somehow seek and win as brothers.

It is the distant neighbor, as well as the one next door, to whom we must give our love. The human family which Christ gathered together in himself, to restore to his Father and ours, can allow no divisions of race or color or nation. We are but one human race created by one God, one family, children of one heavenly Father. So whether in the painful problems and wrongs inside our own homes and our own country or in the complex problems of international politics and world powers, we must work and strive and persevere to make goodness prevail, to make love overcome hatred, by the

power of the goodness and love of the Son of God who came
into our world only for that purpose. We must care, think,
know about, seek out, the troubles and injustices and sorrows
of all, with such a reflection of the saving love of Christ our
Savior that we shall overcome enmity, that we shall enable
and finally compel our politicians and rulers to act as the
ambassadors of the Prince of peace.

7 | Wishes and Facts

"Joy and peace"—these are the special gifts we wish each other at Christmas, and with good reason. It is touching and heartening to see all the wishes and remembrances that people exchange at this season, but it is good to remember that we are not just celebrating a season of good wishes, with their inevitable association of human uncertainty. What we are celebrating at Christmas is not a wish, but a *fulfillment,* a fact of divine certainty. The birth into our humanity of the incarnate Son of God is a blessed reality which is the sure basis of all our human hope and joy and peace. This visible entry of divine love into our world is the great cause of our joy, and gives us every reason to greet each other with peace and happiness.

A sacrament, we learned long ago, is an outward sign of inward grace; and the incarnation of the Son of God is the great sign by which redemptive grace is brought to mankind, the guilt of our sin is washed away, and the abiding presence of God comes to sanctify our whole being. And so we celebrate at Christmas the sacrament of the Incarnation, from which all the seven saving sacraments in Christ's Church draw their power; and when we receive the living body and blood of our Lord in holy communion at Midnight Mass, we raise our hearts sacramentally to meet the charity of God inwardly descending upon us. The event we celebrate at

33

Christmas is a reality, for which we can never cease to thank God. All this is fact, fulfillment, and we hold its truth with the certainty of divine faith.

What, then, of all these *wishes* that we send around so busily at this season? They are wishes that each one may experience the blessed fruit of Christ's presence in his own heart and soul and life. Now that word "experience" can be understood in different ways. First there is the obvious and usual meaning, in the sense of experiencing something con-sciously. This we certainly do mean in our wishes: that others may have something of the joy and peace of Christ's incarnation consciously known and felt in their hearts; that others may realize and enjoy his love, his goodness, his tender care; that others may have a "happy" Christmas.

But there is another sense in which the fruit of the Incar-nation comes to us, one not "experienced" in the way just mentioned. The depth of God's love for us, the fullness of Christ's atonement, the abiding of his Holy Spirit in us— these great realities are not dependent on or limited by the extent of our conscious awareness, let alone our emotional enjoyment of them. While it is sometimes helpful and consol-ing to experience the conscious and sensible joys of our reli-gion, yet these are by no means the whole of it. The real essence of religion is the presence and operation of God in us, and of our will reaching out, often in the dark, to him.

For some time now men have been discovering and prob-ing that mysterious part of our being which they call the subconscious. These gropings beyond the veil that normally limits our consciousness have perhaps not yet grasped any-thing very solid, but they have helped us to realize how many hidden depths there are in this human personality of ours. Some of the elements of our character and our motivation that the psychiatrists are finding in our subconscious turn out to be rather distressing and humiliating, and we could easily begin to be fearful of those depths in our being. But let us remember that God is there too. Deep down in the inmost heart of our being, God abides, in the redemptive grace of Christ, in the creative love of the Holy Spirit. Our whole existence has been consecrated and sealed as his own, by the inward grace which goes far, far more deeply and is far more lasting than the outward sign.

It may be true that most of our time on this earth we have to be thinking of how we can let the divine presence within us come to guide and dominate more and more our conscious life and actions. But at Christmas time let us specially remember, for our consolation and peace, that he whose visible birth we celebrate dwells just as truly, even though invisibly and unfelt, in the deep and hidden recesses of our soul. Even there where we know not ourselves, God knows and abides and sanctifies. No need to lose heart, then, at times when we feel little sensible devotion, little "enjoyment" of religion. The feelings, and even the understanding, are not the main part. The real wonder is that God has come to us, God dwells in us, God works and lives in us and we in him. It is this that we are thanking him for at Christmas; and while we do wish each other all the peace and joy that are the overflow of this holy season, yet the *real* wish is that he may come to us and dwell in us more and more, by faith, by hope, by charity.

8 | The Image and Likeness of Man

When we try to think about our religious belief, we may find to our surprise that the biggest mystery is not God but ourselves. We may possibly find it easier to accept the existence of God than to understand what possible reason could have moved that transcendent Being to call into existence creatures so utterly imperfect compared to himself. Without really attempting to solve that mystery of infinite love, I would suggest a thought which in a way only deepens the mystery, yet also makes it much more beautiful, much more truly divine. It is this: God created man, and all man's universe, precisely in order that God might unite man to himself in the Incarnation.

This design was to be fulfilled, first, in the supreme way of the personal union of human nature with the eternal Word of God in the man Christ Jesus and then, secondly, through that same incarnate God-Man, in drawing all men and women to divine life. The Incarnation was not an advent in the sense of adventitious; the supernatural vocation of man was not a happy afterthought. From the beginning, human nature was created to be open, open to divine union, open to the creative love which makes us sharers of the divine nature. God did not become man just because the men he had created happened to be in need of redemption. Rather, he created man because he intended from the beginning to share divine life and love with man through the Incarnation.

We rightly recognize the incarnation of the Son of God as a most wonderful revelation of God himself to us. How else could we know the divine nature except through him who is the way, the truth, the life? How else could we come to know, not the god of philosophers, but the God and Father of our Lord Jesus Christ? But we should also recognize the Incarnation as an equally wonderful revelation of our own nature to us, a revelation of man's divine vocation and purpose, a revelation of the deep truth in the human mystery and destiny.

If we believe by the grace of Christian faith that the eternal Word of God, the Second Person of the Trinity, took our human nature to himself in living personal union, then we can begin to understand what kind of being man really is. We begin to know what he can be and should be, what he was created to be, what the mind and heart of God conceived him to be. Man was made for God, for divinity. Is this beyond belief? It is certainly beyond imagination, beyond reason and worldly wisdom, beyond all experience. But, please God, not beyond the gift of supernatural faith, not beyond the power of that infinite living Love we call God. Every page of sacred scripture proclaims this to us, heralds a whole new way of being, declares us citizens of the kingdom, children and heirs of the household of God.

This marvelous vocation of humanity was fulfilled uniquely and transcendently once in our history by the hypostatic union of divine nature with our human nature, historically incarnate in the person of Jesus Christ, true God and true man. But the divine plan, and even the divine incarnation, in a wider sense, was not limited to that blessed portion of our humanity we call Jesus. In him and through him all human nature, every man and woman born into this world, is called to share the divine heritage. The blessed life of the Trinity is communicated through Christ to all who unite themselves to him by faith and love; and baptism is the ordinary sacramental sign of this acceptance and incorporation. "You know well enough," the Apostle Paul exclaims, "that we who were taken up into Christ by baptism have been taken up, all of us, into his death. In our baptism, we have been buried with him, died like him, that so, just as Christ was raised up by his Father's power from the dead, we too might live and move in a new kind of existence."

All things therefore are to be restored in Christ, and he is to be all in all. He is not only our Redeemer but also, in the beautiful words of the Apostle, our firstfruits, our firstborn. We are to follow him and be fashioned in his likeness. In him we are to find the true meaning of our humanity, what it means now to be a man, the true revelation of God's plans for our nature. As expressed by the Council Fathers, in the Dogmatic Constitution on the Church: "The followers of Christ are called by God, not according to their accomplishments, but according to His own purpose and grace. They are justified in the Lord Jesus, and through baptism sought in faith they truly become sons of God and sharers in the divine nature. In this way they are really made holy. Then, too, by God's gifts they must hold on to and complete in their lives this holiness which they have received . . . Thus it is evident to everyone that all the faithful of Christ of whatever rank or status are called to the fullness of the Christian life and to the perfection of charity. By this holiness a more human way of life is promoted even in this earthly society." (Par. 40.)

Christian faith is anything but a lessening of our humanity. Men need fear no diminution in accepting Christ's yoke. On the contrary, Christian faith proclaims a destiny and a fulfillment for our nature so sublime as to be incredible except by the help of the Holy Spirit of God in faith. The true meaning and purpose of our human nature is revealed only in the humanity of Christ. There alone do we see, not only the image and likeness of God, but the true image and likeness of man. And the unceasing grace and challenge of Christian life, for every man and woman until the end of time, is to put on Christ.

Epiphany and the New Year

9 | All Time and All the Ages

At the beginning of the year some churches observe an old custom which in the strictly liturgical sense is really a very minor act, yet has a deeply moving significance and comfort. After the Gospel the cantor solemnly sings the actual dates upon which the great "movable feasts" of Christ's saving mysteries will fall this year. Ash Wednesday and the season of Lent, Easter, the Ascension, Pentecost, Corpus Christi —the dates of all these are carefully and joyfully proclaimed. And thus the year is signed and sealed with the sacramental grace of the Incarnation and Redemption: it is a year of the Lord.

How good it is to realize that this world, this time of ours, is indeed now consecrated and sanctified, that we are to work out our salvation in the realities of our daily life, of our common humanity. This is not to forget all those warnings and exhortations about despising the world, turning from the world, even hating the world. But these really refer to the false values of worldliness, the values which reject the transforming grace of Christ, the darkness which knows him not. Jesus came not to destroy the world but to save it. The very name Jesus means Savior, Savior of the world. God so loved the world that he gave his only Son. It is not exactly that salvation is won *from* the world (though we have to think of

43

it that way sometimes), but that salvation is won *for* the world, for the world of mankind, for us.

It is that same world that God first created and saw to be good (because he made it good). Then, by man's rejection of love, there entered into creation sin, evil, death, frustration, loneliness, confusion. But Jesus came precisely to save and to free, to restore life, to bring to man more abundant life, holiness, and fellowship with God that "God may be all in all." By his triumph over the powers that held the world in the helpless bondage of sin, Christ established the kingdom of God in the world. His victory is now so real, the presence of grace so pervading, that "to those who love God all things work together unto good." But the natural conditions of this world remain, and the effects and wounds of sin in our human nature remain; and although our life and work and the things around us are transformed into the ordinary occasions of grace and salvation, yet this is now achieved with much labor and pain for us, as it was for Christ himself who transformed them.

The deep realities of our relation with God by faith and grace are often restless under the burden of external things, and seem to strive to leave them behind. But, paradoxically, the very things which cause us frustration and suffering are the actual means and instruments to be used for salvation. Often in the history of religious experience men have tried to go to God without the intermediary of church, priesthood, sacrament, commandment, dogma. They have wanted to be purely "spiritual," dependent only on "inner light," not on externals of any kind; they have minimized institutions and tried to ignore the instrumentality of the body, of physical things. But the attempt has always ended in delusion, aberration, and failure. There has to be deep humility and patience in man's seeking for God and for godliness. Otherwise, he falls into the tragic original error of the pride that tempts: "You shall be as gods"; he seeks a self-godliness, a false god. True godliness comes through that humble patient faith by which we know that God is "all in all." Then he is God in us too: "By faith we are made sharers of the divine nature."

But these divine gifts are to be received in humility and truth according to the nature he has given to us and redeemed for us. We are not angels, but men; we are not yet in eternity, but in time; we are to work out our salvation in fear and trembling with the ordinary means he has given to us. Christ came into our world and into our humanity, not to destroy but to fulfill them, not to take away their reality and beauty and truth but to teach us to find their true reality and true purpose in the light of their eternal ends. He takes up our time into his timelessness: "Christ yesterday and today, the beginning and the end, Alpha and Omega. All time belongs to him, and all the ages." He leaves us not a man-centered, self-centered world, but a God-centered world. Our year is now truly a year of the Lord; our week turns on the Lord's day; our whole life looks toward his hour, when God will be "all in all."

Our world and our humanity are not to be despised or minimized; rather, we are to see in them the meaning and purpose that faith teaches. Hence we pray, "Thy kingdom come." Christ has established God's kingdom on our earth, but it is always in a state of beginning, always to be more and more recognized and accepted in men's hearts. When men come *really* to accept the kingdom of God and give themselves wholly to his will, then that *is* heaven. And this is the whole purpose of Christ's kingdom on earth in all its elements: his Church, his sacraments, his gospel, his priesthood, his living word. Christ calls men to faith, to see and live and act in the light of eternity, to see the world as God's world, with heavenly holy purposes. Our daily work, our family life, our friendships, our joys, our sorrows, our time, our travel—all are now to be ways toward God, all is now grace. As St. Paul exhorts: "Whether you eat or drink, or whatsoever else you do, do all to the glory of God." And again: "Whatever you are about, in word and action alike, invoke always the name of the Lord Jesus Christ, offering your thanks to God the Father through him."

Until the hour of the Lord comes, then, the kingdom of God is to be fulfilled on earth in patience and in labor, in faith and hope and love. The joy of heaven will come with the passing away of externals and intermediaries, of knowing as we know now. And the eternal knowing will somehow be both a totally new and glorious revelation of the divine beauty, yet also a tender and loving recognition of a familiar friend: "It was You all the time!" Then, at last, God's will will be done "as it is in heaven." Filled with heartfelt assent and joy, we shall truly realize that God is "all in all."

10 | You Have Kept the Good Wine until Now

We find a deep instinct in us, at solemn seasons of the year and at our special "milestones," to wish and to hope for happiness for ourselves and for those we love. This is really much more than some incurably optimistic trait in our humanity. If it were only that, we might well be tempted to discouragement as each year brings its burden of problems and unhappiness. It is really our Christian faith that sees each year open up as a new year of the Lord, a year of hope, and, in spite of all the problems, a year of happiness because Christ himself has entered into our time and filled it with grace.

One of the Sundays early in the year brings us the lovely story of our Lord's first miracle at the wedding feast at Cana. We hear again, as we labor under the burdens of our time, the words with which the wondering steward symbolizes the constant renewal and refreshment of divine grace working in our humanity: "You have kept the best wine until now." This is really the exact opposite of worldly ways. In how many of our endeavors do we start off with the best, but soon lapse into second-best. But the power and love of the Spirit of God never flag; in that power and love are always new wine, new life, filled with refreshment and hope.

We know, of course, that in one sense each new year will bring us the same old world, the same old life, the same old

47

selves. The conditions of our existence here in this world are
always going to be imperfect, always going to bring their
burdens. Yet we are still right in hoping for happiness, because God's providence turns even the limitations of creation
to good ends. This world is not *merely* a place of trial, not
merely something that we have to travel through as best we
can. It has a much more positive reality and blessedness now.
The Son of God himself has entered into our world and consecrated it; our world is now redeemed, now radically holy;
it is now in a wonderful sense full of grace: "To those who
love God all things work together for good." And this means
not only those aspects of our life which are taken and sanctified in some explicit sacramental sense; it concerns also all
those everyday acts and relationships which the incarnate
Word of God touched and entered into, and left no longer
empty but alive with grace and love.

The eternal Word by whom in the beginning all things
were made, he who will come at the end of time for the
heavenly transformation of our world into eternity, that same
Word has entered into our time, becoming man for our salvation. This is the one really new thing, the one really vital
thing that has ever happened, or will ever happen, between
the beginning and the end of time. This is indeed the fullness
of time. Creation was always in God's hands, in God's provi-
dent care and love; but until Bethlehem God's love and word
were made known only indirectly, through the patriarchs and
the prophets. The great phrase of the Old Testament is "God
sent . . ." The wonderful proclamation of the New Testament
is "God comes." He comes now that we may truly know not
his messengers but himself, not just know *about* him but
know him personally in his Son; he comes that we may love
him now in a new way. The gospel proclaims a wholly new

way of being. Our Christian life does not mean simply the correction of faults and the acquisition of virtues, although it does include both of these; it is much more: it is a new revelation, a new creation. Our Christian life is the divine life already at work in us.

Because of Christ's coming, everything is essentially different in this world. The Incarnation not only reveals God to us, but reveals man also. In the divine light of Christ's birth we recognize our own true birth and character as children of God. It is for our sake that he becomes man, in order that we may become what he calls and enables us to be: true children of God. This is the great message of the apostles, the great paschal and pastoral summons to "newness of life." "The Lord is the goal of human history, the focal point of the longings of history and of civilization, the center of the human race, the joy of every heart and the answer to all its yearnings. He it is whom the Father raised from the dead, lifted on high, and stationed at His right hand, making Him Judge of the living and the dead. Enlivened and united in His Spirit, we journey toward the consummation of human history, one which fully accords with the counsel of God's love: 'To re-establish all things in Christ, both those in the heavens and those on the earth' (Eph 1:10)." (Second Vatican Council, Pastoral Constitution on the Church in the Modern World, Par. 45.)

How the coming of Christ has changed this world of ours, how close the Incarnation has brought God to man! The whole purpose of creation was indeed, in the mystery of God's loving kindness, that man should be near to God, united to God. And the very joy of heaven will be precisely the perfect fulfillment of that divine love in the bliss of union. But here on earth, ever since sin disordered creation,

God must be a hidden God, a God to be sought and known by faith and hope; and even our love of him is fulfilled more in sacrifice than in union. This is the long way back to God after man's fall from grace and holiness. Yet God desired and wonderfully managed to give our way back to him a kind of easiness, sureness, swiftness, and joy; he came himself to be our way, our life, to be one of us, close to us, dear and familiar to us. What other way than this way of the Incarnation, this coming of infinite love, could have served to bridge the awful distance between God and man, to bring God so close to us? It is this that gives us strength and hope and joy to face a new year, because he comes to us again in it. It is another year of the Lord, a year of grace, a year of incarnate love. Somehow we humbly trust all things in this new year will work together for our good because of the love which he pours out in our hearts through his Holy Spirit. Somehow we know he has kept the good wine to the last.

11 | The Right Hand of God

How deep and true is the Christian sense of the need for, and the value of, the prayer of intercession; yet how superficial and vague our practice of it sometimes becomes. But there is a vivid and wonderful symbol recurring in the Church's prayer during these weeks following the Epiphany: "the right hand of God." As the Messiah takes up his mission, we are aware of a divine power that has entered into our world for its salvation. By his word and by his miracles a new force and a new hope have come among mankind. "The right hand of the Lord has worked wonders; the right hand of the Lord has saved me; I shall not die but live, and proclaim the works of the Lord" (Offertory Verse, Third Sunday after Epiphany). And the Collect for the same Mass begs that the divine hand may stretch forth its strong protection over us: "Almighty, ever-living God, look mercifully upon our weakness, and stretch forth the right hand of thy majesty to protect us."

No need for us here to concern ourselves over philosophical difficulties about the relationship between our changing prayers and God's infinitely wise and unchanging will. These difficulties arise when we try to see the eternal acts of God in terms of our own familiar dimension of time. But with God there is no past or future; all is present, and our prayers are present to him as part of the eternal designs of his providence. Nor is there really a problem about the causal effect of our prayers upon God's immutable will. Again this arises because we see causality only in terms of our own dependent being and doing. God's creative deed embraces all being and doing in a far more generous and integral way. He created us in his own image and likeness, sharing with us something of creativity itself. He made us his agents, not just his puppets, not really passive but truly animated with life and power.

Man has thus been graced by God with the great dignity and the great responsibility of a living creative personality. Man responds to this responsibility both by his acts and by his prayer. This is one reason why it is important that our petitions be not so general that they involve no real mental energy on our part. Vague generalized prayer, which just drops a jumble of needs into God's hands hoping that he will do something about it, lacks some very significant factors. It is not, of course, that God needs any specifics, but that some true human mental energy and specific attention are needed on our side, both that we may "do what in us lies" and also that we may be better disposed to receive the answers God may grant us. It may be, for instance, precisely our petitions and dispositions that God's providence wills to use as part of the means of fulfilling our prayer. So it is not only that one hopes that a greater intensity of beseeching would be, as it were, brought to bear to influence God, but also that a more responsible and effective thinking and acting would be brought about by such prayer on the human side of the relationship. That is, that we may fulfill worthily our tremendous but wonderful vocation as free and responsible agents in the living design of God's providence.

Fortunately, our Christian prayer does not depend on our laborious reasoning to justify its reality and its role. The incarnate Son of God both prayed himself and taught us to pray. Prayer is now part of revelation, part of our Christian life and duty. Even our most material and human needs are to be prayed about: "Give us this day our daily bread"; "Ask and you shall receive." True, prayer at its purest and highest may attain great simplicity and detachment from earthly busyness; that is when it is catching a reflection of the pure beauty and bright simplicity of God himself. But prayer will also rightly have its complexities and its multiplicity of needs, of soul and body, heart and mind, because in these it is reflecting our humble human reality, our proper dependence on God.

By such prayer we are not really trying to change God's will to ours, but to change and unite our will to his. We need not even put it in those terms, for we are trying to fulfill a wonderful mutual enterprise. In this partnership the One to whom we pray is infinite wisdom, infinite love, infinite goodness. But that does not destroy the truth and reality of our part; for he himself gives us of his own goodness and wisdom; nevertheless, it is the reason why all our petitions end with the unspoken prayer "Not my will but thine."

Why, then, any petition at all? Why not leave it all to him who knows all of us and all our needs? Because he knows us not as things, but as persons. We are meant to be in God's knowledge, not merely as rocks and trees are known to him, but as he created us in his own image and likeness: as persons, knowing that they are known, and willing to be known. Indeed, it is even more than this, for in the Holy Spirit of God himself we have been taught to cry Abba, Father. Thus shall you pray: "Our Father . . ." Therefore, we rightly offer to him all our hopes and fears, all our sorrows and desires. To whom else should we go?

Septuagesima

12 | Spiritual Shadowboxing

G. K. Chesterton, in a characteristic passage, describes the course of the Church as a wonderful careering, zigzag process through the centuries. We do not need much knowledge of history, or psychology, or theology, to appreciate the truth of his observation. The course of our religious thought and action has not followed some lifeless mechanical rule dead straight down the middle of human history, but has been a living part of human history, sharing mankind's existence and vicissitudes. Not that divine truth changes or that good becomes evil, but in each generation the mind of man must grapple with that truth with his own finite faculties, must reach out to that goodness from his own sincere conscience. And because man is always limited and inadequate in his efforts, it will be the heritage of each generation to correct and amplify the understanding of the last; yet, in so doing, each generation itself inevitably falls short in some way. All this is really proof of life and reality in our encounter with the infinite. There would be something manifestly false about a system of thought that claimed to have complete comprehension of the divine. Always there will remain the invitation to deepen, clarify, purify, our joyful knowledge of inexhaustible truth and beauty.

It is very clear that we are in a movement of very strong zigging and zagging in this generation of the Church's life.

Most of us are joyfully convinced that we are witnessing a marvellous stirring of Christ's Church by the power of his Spirit; and we are not too disconcerted if, along with the vital renewal, there are some regrettable aberrations in thought and even in conduct. The divine force moves in actual human beings, and we must expect some human error and even perversity. God's great works, while they are truly his free gifts, always have a do-it-yourself character about them; he has made men so much more than puppets; he has made them truly to live and act in his own image and likeness.

Is it not something of this kind that the liturgy of Septuagesima is all about? If we may venture to say so, the Church suddenly gets a lot more practical in her message to us. To oversimplify things, we might say that until now the Church's prayers and thought have been mainly joyfully contemplative and even slightly idealistic. We have only to contemplate peacefully the wondrous mystery of the Incarnation, the embodiment of infinite love descending upon our humanity. And even if the Epiphany period indeed proclaimed a great call to us to recognize the Messiah and to respond by faith to his word, yet it was, if I may dare to say so, all a little bit up in the air, all a little bit taken for granted in the first great flush of joyful revelation: "Come and hear, all you who fear God, while I tell you what great things he has done for my soul." The happy Christian seems to be rather taking the promise for fulfillment, the sublime possibilities of the divine plan for actualities. Then suddenly, if we may speak so irreverently of the ship of Peter, the Church lowers the boom. Septuagesima Sunday really brings us down, down to face our human condition as it really is here and now: fallen, sinful, weak. And in the anguish of reaction we cry out in the words of the Introit: "The groans of death surrounded me; the sorrows of hell encompassed me. In my affliction I called upon the Lord, and he heard my voice from his holy temple." The scripture lessons in this Mass provide the salutary instruction. The Gospel narrative of the laborers in the vineyard does indeed remind us that our reward lies wholly in God's gift, but all the same it teaches us that we are called to *labor* in the vineyard. And much more pointedly in the Epistle, St. Paul reminds us that our Christian life is a race to be run, a battle to be fought.

St. Paul uses a figure that would be familiar and convincing to his people at Corinth, which was one of the centers for the great athletic contests like the present-day Olympic Games. And even to our own unathletic selves, how that metaphor hits home! Is our Christian life an all-out race, or are we sauntering along with many a detour or even retreat? Are we really attacking the enemy, or are we wasting our blows upon the air? But why, we weakly protest, would we do that? The answer is because that enemy, the person we are struggling with, is ourself. And we take good care that while we do a lot of flailing and swinging, like an old-fashioned movie fight, no very effective blow is ever allowed to land where it would hurt, on our precious self. What a lot of clever shadowboxing we are able to display in the religious ring, without ever getting within striking range!

But, St. Paul says, this won't do. We are not going to win this contest by feints and self-deceits. He warns that our forefathers were also given the benefit of God's special signs and graces: the pillar of cloud, the passage through the Red Sea, the manna, the miraculous water from the rock; "but with most of them God was not well pleased." We must overcome that dangerous weakness we have, that inclination to substitute religious "things" for personal worship of God in spirit

and in truth, that tendency to trust in observance rather than
in the essential love. We cheerfully despise the Pharisees, and
fail to recognize how much we all share their fatal error. But
Christ himself has taught us clearly that there is only one
supreme rule of life: to love the Lord God with our whole
heart. What this beautiful but difficult commandment means,
what it must require from our weak sinful nature, is the great
saving lesson of Lent—as the Church leads us to share in the
perfect oblation of Christ, toward which our whole gaze is
now turned.

Lent

13 | The Spirit of Lent

It is natural and proper that the penitential season should inspire us with a certain reasonable awe and fear; this is a hopeful sign that it does really mean something to us. But, in another way, I think we may feel a sort of relief. Wonderful as it is to dwell in the joyful, contemplative seasons of the year, we may yet have a little feeling in the back of our mind that these heights are a bit too sublime for us, that we are not yet fully at home in these high places. And, instinctively, as we are guided by the Church into a realistic, practical time like Lent, we recognize that here we have something more clearly adapted to our immediate and obvious needs. We know that here we are being helped and invited by the Church to tackle what in practice is always a first and inescapable step; to loosen the bonds of our sins.

The dramatic character of the beginning of the penitential season has often been remarked. One can hardly miss it, with that Introit which introduces it at Septuagesima: "The groans of death surrounded me; the sorrows of hell encompassed me . . ." It is the cry of the human heart as it begins to understand the reality of the following of Christ, the cost of redemption. The wonderful fact of the Incarnation has the tremendous corollary that man is to be made a sharer in the divine life; and this can only be done through sharing in the suffering of Christ, through dying with him to sin, that we may rise with him in newness of life. Our poor fallen nature has to be utterly transformed: no mere superficial piety, but a radical operation that the scriptures call "dying daily," that concerns our most personal self, our most selfish personality. "For the word of God is living and effectual, and more piercing than any two-edged sword; and reaching unto the division of the soul and the spirit, of the joints also and the marrow, and is a discerner of the thoughts and intents of the heart."

But if the message of this season is precisely a call to penance, to prayer, to fasting, especially to the great fast from sin, and to the reordering of our whole life in the supernatural light of grace and truth, yet it is important to notice the *spirit* of this call. The right approach to penitence and the cross is not from any spirit of dejection, not from morbid self-disgust, not from over-intense preoccupation with our sins, our worthlessness, our danger. This would make a very weak and changeable foundation for our efforts, and would give us very little hope of perseverance. No, the spirit of Lent is other than this. While the Church calls us to penance, to self-denial, to the recognition of the cross and its message (and her call is indeed clear and firm), she also teaches and helps us to respond to it in a spirit of cheerful hope, great trust, peaceful resignation.

In this frame of mind, a man can face his difficulties and can persevere in bearing them. He is not defeated and discouraged but, even in failure, struggles on again with a fresh start. This spirit opens the way for God's power to triumph in our weakness. On the First Sunday of Lent the one theme of Introit, Gradual, Tract, Offertory, and Communion is that verse from Psalm 90: "The Lord will overshadow you with his shoulders, and under his wings you shall trust; his truth shall compass you with a shield." The first reference here is to the incident of the temptation of our Lord, which the Gospel of this Mass narrates; but surely it is meant to inspire the mood of our prayer too. Or recall that verse which the Church uses several times during the first days of Lent: "When I cried to the Lord he heard my voice . . . cast your care upon the Lord, and he will sustain you." Or the Introit of Ash Wednesday itself: "You have mercy on all, O Lord, and hate none of the things which you have made, overlooking the sins of men for the sake of repentance, and sparing them."

More and more one is struck by the prominence of joy, hope, peace, confidence, in the Lenten liturgy. We have seen the wonder of the Incarnation; then we have seen the terrible depths of sin; we cry out our *De profundis;* and we turn after all with peace and hope back to God, our firmament and our refuge. This is the final disposition with which we enter upon the holy season of Lent, and place ourselves in his saving, purifying hands: "Now is the acceptable time, now is the day of salvation."

14 | Death, Where Is Your Victory?

"Remember, man, you are but dust, and unto dust you shall return." These are the words we hear on Ash Wednesday as the ashes are placed on our heads in vivid symbol both of penitence and mortality. We have good reasons for the traditional concept of death in terms of sadness and loss, as an evil to be accepted in punishment and consequence of sin. Holy scripture, the Church's liturgical prayer, the writings of the saints, all provide plenty of examples of this approach to death. And it is indeed salutary that we should be humbly conscious of our need for redemption, of our captivity in the bonds of sin, of our subjection to the disintegration and mortality which sin has brought to our nature.

Divine grace and the strong instinct of Christian tradition have made this lesson clear to us, and there is perhaps no need to stress this vivid and inescapable aspect of Christian death. What is useful, I think, is to recall how wonderfully God's loving providence turns all things to good for those who love him, even death itself. It is not without reason that the Apostle Paul exults: "Death is swallowed up in victory. O death, where is your victory? O death, where is your sting?" For death itself, the very consequence of man's sinful disordering of God's creation, becomes a most effective and vital instrument of our liberation from sin, our entry into salvation. In a striking thought, St. Irenaeus, in the second cen-

66

tury of Christian faith, sees death not so much as an act of
divine punishment as of merciful compassion: "It is for pity
that God removed man far away from the tree of life . . . for
fear he might remain a sinner forever and sin become immortal, and evil unending and incurable. So he set a stop to
transgression by interposing death and putting an end to sin
by causing the flesh to decay in the earth, so that man might
in the end cease to live for sin and in dying might begin to
live for God." (Adv. Haer. 3, 23, 6 PG 964 AB.)

Can we imagine this poor life of ours, as it is in its fallen
state on this earth, stretching out endlessly before us, always
incomplete, always unfinished? Surely if there were no sense
of finality, no urgency, no decision, our life would be de-
prived of all motivation, all purpose, all proportion and
value. If we were faced with never-ending time, unlimited
transience and recurrence, never the finality but always the
temporary, we should go mad. There would be no reason to
do anything, to make any choice, to exercise any effort; there
would be total demoralization. Unlimited time would be
worse than no time at all. It would be the end of life before it
ever really began.

The great point and value of Christian death is that it
makes possible an act of decision, of choice. And it is so in a
way quite different from any other act or decision in our life,
even though all these other choices prepare for it. For the
decision made in death is a final decision, and that cannot be
said of any other decision in our life. Every other decision is
subject to the very condition of our life and nature in this
situation of temporariness and alternation, mutability and
imperfection. But with death all these conditions fall away;
man enters at last into the fullness of personal being and
acting. He faces the great choice at death with all the power

and all the inescapability of *the final decision*. He is freed by death from all invasion by the outside world, from social and cultural and psychological influences, from the imprisonment of his own mortality and all its impedimenta. There is nothing left except his personal being; he is free at last to exercise his choice clearly, fully, finally. Nothing else, that is to say, except God; he is now fully open to God: to choose or to reject him.

St. Paul is fond of reminding us that by faith and baptism we are buried with Christ, dead to sin, alive to God. This is the great grace and joy of our Christian newness of life. But, in a way, this only reaches its final fulfillment when we are truly buried with Christ in the act of Christian death—that is, when we have made the great final and irrevocable choice of Christ, accepting the grace of Christian death as the means of surrendering ourselves perfectly at last to his love, in the blessed hope of sharing his risen life.

For while Christian life means to enter into the whole blessed being of Christ, his life and death, his passion and resurrection, yet in one very true sense we are indeed redeemed by Christ's death. For Christ too, in the reality of his humanity, the perfection and fulfillment of his loving oblation and his redemptive work was achieved in the final choice and consummation of his death. For him too, all his life and all its decisions were preparing and leading to this final act of Christian death. Only at that final moment could he say: "It is consummated." Only then did he accomplish his life's mission, in that final and decisive *fiat* of his cross.

There begins, for every follower of Christ, a whole new way of existence when he is buried with Christ in the waters of baptism. He is called then to die to the old life of sinfulness and to walk in divine newness: "You *have* eternal life." But this sublime gift of supernatural life only becomes truly and perfectly ours when it is finally grasped in the final and irrevocable decision of Christian death. Only then can we echo Christ's words: "It is consummated." Only then can we hear the divine acceptance: "Come you blessed of my Father, enter into the kingdom." Whatever other true and salutary meaning death has for the Christian soul then, let us not overlook its character as a very special Christian sacramental sign and instrument of God's redemptive providence. That is why the saints embrace it so joyfully, and say with St. Paul: "To die is gain."

15 | Hearts and Not Garments

"Although our life ought at all times to have a Lenten character, yet since few are strong enough for this, we exhort all, at least during the days of Lent, to keep themselves in all purity of life, and to wash away during this holy season the negligences of other times. This we shall worthily do if we refrain from all sin, and give ourselves to prayer, holy reading, and abstinence, withholding from our body somewhat of our food, drink and sleep, and refraining from talking and mirth. In these days, then, let every one of his own will offer to God, with joy of the Holy Spirit, something beyond the measure appointed him, and await Holy Easter with the joy of spiritual longing." (Rule of St. Benedict, Ch. 49.)

What St. Benedict teaches here is plainly what we ourselves first mean when we think of Lenten observance. Namely, it is an invitation to true self-denial in every sincere way, of body and soul, mind and heart. It is the challenge to a more generous renunciation of all that does not belong to Christ in our life, so that we may be enabled to put on Christ more truly. And this includes some element of bodily mortification because our bodies certainly do make up a very real part of our existence. It is well to start by acknowledging this as honestly as we can, because in fact most of us seem only too ready to minimize the element of bodily mortification in the Christian life. It seems that we are much more willing to stress the importance of interior mortification of the spirit in humility, obedience, patience, charity; and while it is indeed true that these are more essential, more indispensable, it is also true that they can be vague, intangible, delusive. Whatever may be the limitations and dangers of corporal austerities, at least they have a reality and immediacy by which they bring their force to bear upon our sensitive humanity. In any case, we really know that we need some kind of Christian discipline at every level of our nature.

It is rather typical and revealing that everybody is tending to refer to a recent document of Pope Paul as "abolishing" fasting. The simplest attention to its teaching, however, shows immediately that the purpose of this instruction is really exactly the opposite. The Holy Father is insisting most strongly on the special need in our times for Christian penitence in prayer, fasting, and good works. He is pleadng for a renewal and deepening of the spirit of penitence as a vital element in the reform of the Church, the renewal of Christian life, and the preservation of the whole world. What has been abolished, if we can use the word at all, is merely the formal canonical sanction attached to the law of fasting. But it is made clear that this is done mainly in the hope that Christian men and women of good will may take up all the more generously, through a sense of personal responsibility and love, the necessary practice of fasting and abstinence.

In the history of Christian asceticism it is striking to note how the trend has always been to mitigation, never to intensification. Each generation always has, or thinks it has, more than enough material left for its mortification. But I do not think that this is simply a process of corruption or relaxation in the Church. Men who were themselves great ascetics by any standards have played leading roles in this development,

including St. Benedict. He certainly played his part in the
shift of emphasis from external to internal asceticism. In
part, this process seems to be a kind of necessary disentan-
glement or clarification that has to be continually renewed.
We have such a way of identifying means with ends, such an
instinct to settle on material things and practices, to become
dependent on them, to find a false security in them, and to
believe that when we have fulfilled them we have fulfilled
the whole law. And time and time again through salvation
history, both in the Old Testament and in the New, men have
had to learn that it is not in observances, not in religious
practices, that salvation is found, but only in love, in the
worship of God in spirit and in truth. How clearly the Son of
God himself taught this great lesson! Yet how often we all
have to relearn it. How strong in us is that instinct by which
we seek to reduce religion to certain practices, almost tricks,
which we call "attending to our religious duties." We like to
feel that there are a few definite things which we have to do,
such as going to church, contributing to the various drives,
and eating fish; and once we have done these, we are all set!
So the Church is always having to shake us up again: "Rend
your hearts and not your garments . . . Be converted with
your whole heart."

The kingdom of God can be entered only by a change of
heart, that is to say, through that intimate and total change
and renewal of the entire man, of all his opinions, judgments,
and decisions, which take place in him in the light of the
sanctity and charity of God, manifested and communicated in
the Son. That is why there have to be these periods in the
Church's history which seem to bring a rather confusing and
painful breaking up, but which are really meant to lead to a
fresh breaking through. Settled customs have to be reex-

amined with a certain detachment and even ruthlessness. Always we are having to strive to detach ourselves from things, even religious things, to be free for the living God.

But then, having tried to clarify and redirect our thoughts and affections more purely to God alone, the one end, then of course we have to return once more, humbly, realistically, to the means to that one divine end. We have to return to all the things that we have broken away from, or to things very like them, because, quite simply, we need them. We creatures cannot find our way to God in this life without the help of creatures. And with all their disadvantages and dangers we cannot do without their complexities, because we ourselves are so complex. So we turn again, humbly, to try to make good use of all these things, of all these practices, of all these observances. But the hope is that for a while at least, we shall see them more clearly for what they are, means to the end, and use them more wisely for the great purpose of growing in divine love. Therefore, in the instruction of Pope Paul, for example, we are really invited and exhorted to return to fasting, but in the spirit of true Christian love and penitence, sharing in the perfect oblation of Christ, not *merely* for the sake of observance of law, nor with the notion that somehow fish on Friday is the essence of Catholic life.

Similarly, while St. Benedict so wonderfully first liberates his sons from any fanatical yoke of ascetical observance, yet he then exhorts them to the complete putting on of Christ in body and soul in the spirit of love and Christian penitence. In a really profound Lenten spirit, then, let us try to give ourselves generously to prayer, holy reading, and some abstinence in our appetites, offering ourselves willingly with the joy of the Holy Spirit, in union with Christ's own paschal oblation.

16 | Joy of a Child, Joy of a Man

Rather unexpectedly, the customary phrase in Christian tradition is *holy* Lent. We do not seem to say holy Christmas, or holy Pentecost, or holy Epiphany, though these are surely seasons of grace and holiness. Lent is concerned with sorrow for sin, with prayer and fasting, with guilt and redemption, with the passion and death of our Savior. Yet we say holy Lent. But that is precisely the point. We somehow realize that this *is* the season of grace, of redemption; this is the very work of holiness which the Redeemer came to do. It is holy Lent precisely because through the redemptive sacrifice of Christ we are able to await holy Easter with the joy of spiritual longing.

Here is a marvellous example of the triumph of God's wise and loving providence. Out of the very evil of sin and suffering and death is created a new kind of life, a new kind of joy, a new kind of holiness. God's will is never defeated and never spoiled; always its creative love is able to bring about something even better than what might have been. Easter joy is really a much deeper, purer joy than Christmas joy. It might not at first seem so. We might feel that if only the sweetness and tender peace of the Christ Child's birth could have lasted forever, unspoilt by man's rejection and sin, everything would have been perfect. Indeed, in a sense, so it ought to have been. Men ought to have welcomed the Messiah with

74

faith and love, and followed him joyfully into his kingdom of justice and truth and peace. But in fact men rejected and crucified him, and the Savior had to fulfill his redemptive mission by means of loving sacrifice instead of messianic triumph.

But through sacrifice—that is, through the spirit of loving oblation—love is in fact intensified, and joy is finally purified and deepened. What joy can ever be like Easter joy, the joy of the risen Savior himself, and the joy of us his disciples receiving him, recognizing him at last, believing at last, opening our hearts to his redemptive forgiveness at last. "Peace be to you . . . the disciples were filled with joy when they saw the Lord." Only the joy of the heavenly Easter itself can equal this joy. Christmas joy is, however beautiful, however deep and significant, the joy of a child. Easter joy is the joy of a man, a man come to his full stature, matured by sorrow and self-sacrifice, a man who having loved his own loved them to the very end. It is the joy of those who have known what it means to follow Christ, to share his cross, to share by loving oblation his redemptive sacrifice.

To most of us, this kind of deep Christian joy comes only rarely in our lives. Occasionally our souls open to a bright gleam of it, but mostly we are doing well just to struggle to bear our troubles as resignedly and bravely as we can. Over the years I have gradually discovered that there is hardly a family, perhaps hardly a single human person, that is without some grave problem or worry. When we first come to know our friends, we think they are so carefree. As we get to know them better, we find that they may indeed be happy, in a true deep sense, because of their courage and patience and hope and love; but they are certainly not free from care. Sooner or later we learn something of the burden of suffering they bear, whether it be of the body or of the mind or heart or soul. Ever since the radical disorder of sin and rebellion came into our world, some degree of suffering has been part of our human destiny. Even the incarnate Son of God himself, when he came to take our humanity to himself, did not take away our suffering. In a sense he could not, in spite of all the tender love of his sacred heart; suffering is too much part of our reality now. But he did something much more wonderful: he came to share our suffering, and to transform it into the most vital instrument of our redemption. And he invites us most compassionately to share that wonderful means of holiness: "Can you drink the chalice that I shall drink?" Some brave and holy people give everything they have, and drink deeply of the chalice of the Lord's suffering; but all of us have to try to share it as bravely as we can. And the more we learn to give ourselves with love, the more we learn to "let go," the more we shall begin to learn the truth of that other word of holy scripture: "Taste and see, for the Lord is sweet!"

17 | What Might Have Been

The story of Jesus and his teaching is the most beautiful thing in human history. Even if we could not give true faith to it, we should want to cling to it as the most touching and beautiful dream or poem mankind ever knew. And, many levels higher than that of a merely wistful dream, our souls do sense the beauty and attraction of God; we are made in his likeness, and our whole being tends toward him. So it is not really difficult to meditate at times with some pleasure and even fervor on the sublime truths of our faith and the wonderful plans of God for his children.

Then, suddenly we remember sin; and our fervor is chilled. We come down from the clouds of easy holiness to the cold hard earth of our easy sinfulness. And when we begin to realize some of the renunciations that might be required of us, we are tempted to turn our minds away from the thought of higher things, to busy ourselves in many activities. But it is a mistake to be thus scared off the more positive consideration of our great vocation by the half-glimpsed bogey of sin. It is better to have a good hard look at this problem. Certainly it would be a mistake, in this poor somewhat schizophrenic spiritual life of ours, not to attend at all to that heavy foot that tends to drag along in the gutter, while our other foot tries to tread the ways of heaven.

As to the terrible nature of sin itself, its degradation of our

soul, its offense against the infinite holiness of our God, its
danger of eternal damnation, I shall only suggest two consid-
erations. First, the nature of sin is such that it demands the
existence of hell and eternal punishment. Secondly, the price
of our redemption from sin was the crucifixion of the Son of
God. Realization of these two facts ought to bring a more
profound understanding of the character of sin than any
merely imaginative attempt to depict its horrors.

But let us rather consider more practically and personally,
not sin in general, but our own sins and sinfulness in particular. And perhaps we may find that we are not faced with such
a hopelessly depressing obstacle to God's grace and love as we
are at first tempted to feel.

First, there are our past sins. Or rather, there are not our
past sins. For they are past; they do not any longer exist.
Need they really be an obstacle to our love of God now? Or
can they not rather serve as a help, by leading us to humility,
sorrow, gratitude, and trust? Rather than dwelling on our
past sins in themselves, we can make better use of the past in
a different way, by humbly, sorrowfully recognizing the good
we missed, what might have been. Each of us gets a glimpse
at times of what *I*, even I, might have been, with just a little
faithfulness and generosity in responding to grace. We can
almost see the sort of person God meant us to be—the same
person, but so much finer, truer, more consistent, more lov-
able. Not just the person I should have been, but the person I
really could have been—even I! Instead, there was an idle,
reckless squandering of grace, an irresponsible temporizing
with temptation and sin, a senseless dulling of that reflection
of God's goodness and truth that he intended me to be, but
I just could not be bothered.

Perhaps that sort of realization, even more than the recol-

lection of particular sins, may move us to true sorrow for our
faithless neglect of grace and to more generous resolve for the
future.

Then there is the future. Again we are tempted to dejection and discouragement. We shall certainly fall into sin
again; what is the use of these moods of fervor and optimism?
To be honest, can we really pretend that we even want to cut
off our sins for the future? For today, yes—while we are in
these good circumstances or this good mood. Do we not try,
however, to leave a little line of communication open somewhere, a little loophole, so that when the moment comes we
shall in fact be able to indulge our poor weakness? But is
there any point at all in thinking and worrying about the
future? We do not even know whether there will be a tomorrow for us; and if there is, its conditions may be very different
from what we foresee. It is true that we shall be sinners until
our death; but future sin can only be left to God's future
grace and mercy. We do not have to answer now for the
future, except insofar as we are really making or willing that
future now.

The only real question about sin, then, is the present. And
perhaps, even here, it is not just our actual poor sins that we
have to consider, but our attitude about sin. In a way, our
actual sins are but the external symptoms, the clues, that
reveal what we are. They betray the habitual disposition and
tending of our soul—either pointing truly toward God, or
perversely toward our own desires. Or perhaps they indicate
our inconsistency, our erratic insensitiveness and indifference
toward God.

Are we not conscious of something like this? Yet we can
sometimes hardly believe it of ourselves. Our life doesn't
seem to make sense. If our sins are grave, how could we so

grievously turn away from our God? If our sins are petty, how could we so lightly, heedlessly fail in so slight an effort toward grace? When I recall the special providence with which God has led me since childhood, and especially his constant mercy and forgiveness after my falls, I see not only my sins, but a sinful indifference and carelessness deep in myself. So little concern whether I offend or not, whether I give scandal or not.

What is the order in my life, the real order, not the order professed in my prayers? What really comes first? Is it not my self-indulgence, my sloth, my pride, my ambition, my vanity, my cheap shallow satisfactions? Yet this soul of mine, this immortal person that I am, was called out of nothingness by sheer love, was elevated to supernatural life by the incarnate Son of God, can be nourished daily by his living body and blood. All this, just to amount to what I am now? Am I not cheaply trying to have it both ways: hoping to save my soul somehow, but slipping into any devious way that seems to half excuse the selfish satisfactions of the moment?

And thus we are led to the awakening graces of penitence, to deeper sorrow, to more effective amendment of our lives. In the great penitential Psalm 50, the *Miserere,* we pray that a steadfast spirit be renewed in us. May we be truly renewed with a clear, strong, serious purpose in life, one to be kept steadily in mind and aimed at day by day. Lord, that I may see! Lord, that I may follow you! Lord, that I may be what you mean me to be!

18 | The Forgiveness of Sins

When we say that great profession of our faith, the Apostles' Creed, we start off rather solemnly and deliberately: "I believe in God the Father almighty, Creator of heaven and earth. And in Jesus Christ his only Son our Lord, who was conceived by the Holy Spirit, born of the Virgin Mary . . ." But by the time we reach the end, we are gabbling great truths of our faith in a breathless blur as though they were a multiplication table: " . . . the Holy Spirit, the holy Catholic Church, the communion of saints, the forgiveness of sins, the resurrection of the body and life everlasting. Amen." If we really took time to consider what we are saying in these last wonderful proclamations, we should end not with "Amen" but with "Hooray!"

For now, let us try to rescue just one of those tremendous truths: the forgiveness of sins. Sometimes we are amused, or pretend to be, at the way some people misunderstand Catholic belief about the forgiveness of sins. They think that we believe in a kind of license to commit sin or, at least, in a kind of easy out afterward. But do we ourselves really understand the doctrine of forgiveness of sin very profoundly? What about the notion of a mechanical "going to confession" which blurs the sharp outlines of right and wrong, so that we all too easily slip in and out of grace and sin, all too easily feel ourselves absolved from wrongdoing? The sacrament of penance does not really say, "Never mind, it does not really matter, just fill out the usual form . . ." Sin always matters, terribly, and the sacrament is not intended to make light of sin. That is just our usual characteristic human misunderstanding and abuse of good things, including God's good things. Such a notion of forgiveness would fail to understand on the one hand the sublime reality of the moral order and our personal responsibility toward it, and on the other hand the creative power of divine forgiveness.

On our side, sacramental confession is not given to us as a substitute for true sorrow. It is given to us as a wonderfully effective means to help us to recognize our sin, to judge it, to be truly sorry for it, and to take sincere steps to avoid repeating it. Any Christian soul that approaches this sacrament sincerely knows from experience how true this is, how much more effective is this sacramental help than any *merely* private good intentions of our own. Penance bestows actual grace in the supernatural order and, at the same time, employs wise means in the natural order—mainly psychological: recognition, confession, judgment, guidance, reparation—to bring about the effective amendment of our life.

But the sacrament does more than this. It leads our repentance in a special way to the living creative forgiveness of God. It does not just deny or conceal our guilt; it "confesses" it, brings it to the light, to the truth, to the loving merciful ever-creative power of God. This repentance is itself a grace and a gift of God; and it is met by the divine power that first drew man out of nothingness into being. That same power now draws man out of the nothingness of sin into newness of life, divine life, holiness, communicated from the inexhaustible source of holiness and life which is God himself. Then our sin no longer exists. The human act which was sin's vesture, the act of theft or lust or hatred, is a historical fact recorded indelibly in time and place, and may indeed leave its sad effects behind it in the life of ourselves or of others. But the sin itself, the bad will and malice, the loss of divine grace, the separation from God, all that is gone, swept away by the grace of repentance and forgiveness. There has been the mystery of creation once more: God has drawn the sinner to himself, to give him new life, new hope. "You will turn to us and give us life . . . . And your people will rejoice in you."

19 | Blessed Is the Man Who Is Not Scandalized in Me

It seems important these days to keep very much in mind those strange and striking words of our Lord to John the Baptist: "Blessed is the man who is not scandalized in me." In the weeks before Passiontide the liturgy itself describes the tension building up between the Messiah and the establishment represented by the Scribes and Pharisees; and men are more and more confronted with the choice they must make in accepting or rejecting the Savior. The conflict is soon to reach its tragic climax in the scandal of the cross.

We should note first that although our Lord sternly rebukes abuses, he does not in fact separate himself from the institution. He allows himself to be rejected and condemned; but he himself does not defect from the official church. Indeed, every act of his life, of his passion, death, and resurrection, is offered that the law and the prophets may be fulfilled. To the very end his prayer is for his people, the chosen people of God. On Good Friday, as we venerate his cross, the Church puts on his lips the moving cry: "My people, what have I done to you, or in what have I grieved you?" It is not Jesus who has rejected his people, but his people who have rejected him.

But I am really thinking of those words of our Lord to John the Baptist in a more practical sense, applying them to

84

our own personal life and attitude in these days of post-conciliar growing pains. For if the incarnate Son of God himself, in his own sacred person, in all his holiness and truth and beauty, had to warn men not to be scandalized, not to lose faith in him, is it any wonder that his much *more* incarnate mystical body (if we may express it in that way) should present the temptation of scandal a hundredfold?

Surely there is no reason for too much shock in this. If the Son of God had to reassure and confirm St. John against the temptation of doubt and scandal in his own immediate person, how much more should we expect this in his Church, his mystical body, which we ourselves constitute? In the Church the truth and holiness of God are indeed made known to men of good will. But how much they are also concealed and distorted, not now merely by the sinless humanity of Christ himself, but by the sinful humanity of us all. And, from the very nature of things, must we not expect the difficulties to be more visible in the weaknesses and failures of those to whom authority is committed?

So although we may suffer bitter disappointment and sorrow, we must surely not take excessive and unrealistic scandal at the human failures within the Church of Christ. If these were not present, could we really believe that his mystical body was truly embodied in *us?* "Blessed is the man who is not scandalized in me." Surely our merciful Redeemer was saying this even more for the sake of his mystical body than for himself. While for us, however troubled and scandalized we may sometimes feel, our final, decisive, perhaps sometimes almost desperate, answer to the Lord in his Church will always be: "To whom else should we go? You have the words of eternal life."

Religion is the meeting of God and creature, of infinite

holiness and ingrained sinfulness. It is both revelation and mystery. What can it be but a sign of contradiction? We may see it typified in the luminous cloud which was so often the sign of the presence of God among men. It is both light and shadow. It led the Israelites through the desert and marked the presence of God over the ark of the covenant; yet the unbelievers scoffed at the people who worshiped an empty shrine. It was the bright cloud that overshadowed the disciples at the transfiguration of Jesus; yet when they raised their eyes they saw only Jesus. In the humanity of Christ divine revelation was wonderfully made to mankind; and yet at the same time the humanity of Jesus was a kind of concealing of the Godhead. Christ's living reality in flesh and blood was both a scandal to men and a challenge and grace to men of good will. "It has been granted to you to know the secrets of the kingdom of heaven, but to those others it has not been granted . . . for they look without seeing, and listen without hearing or understanding." And the same paradox is clearly found in the Holy Eucharist, in which the signs of bread and wine conceal from our eyes, yet focus and manifest to our faith, the glorious action and presence of Christ.

Certainly this paradox is present and inescapable in the whole Church of Christ on earth. We all recognize this. What we find difficult, however, is to apply it to all the lesser institutions within the Church, which are in fact real and living cells and members of the mystical body. It applies also, for example, to marriage and family life, to the priesthood and religious life, and to many other states of life. There too, the sacrifice of faith and the sometimes painful courage of hope may be very real.

So it seems to me that, besides all those extra good works which we may have proposed for ourselves at the beginning of Lent, we have in fact a very clear and vital Lenten work cut out for us this year and perhaps for many years to come. It is the supreme and essential work of giving ourselves with deeper faith and braver hope to the bond of charity in the mystical body. The great challenge of these days of renewal and reform is the call to charity and unity—not to draw apart from one another, but to draw closer together, and, above all, closer in our unity in the church of Christ. One Lord, one faith, one baptism. We can only help in the vital unceasing work of reform and renewal from *within*. And this is true in the deepest sense, not in some technical legal sense, but in truly being within the Church in sincere and generous love and faith and patient hope.

This does not mean, of course, some kind of false loyalty, or flattering, "spoiling" love. Our Lord spoke out in protest and rebuke against the abuses in the institution of his time; conscience always comes first, obedience to God first. And there is always the danger of making mistakes; but, as the Superior General of the Jesuits has recently pointed out, the biggest mistake of all is to fail to attempt anything, for fear of making a mistake. What we must try to be sure of is that we speak and act in *true* love, *true* faith: that our love is always greater than our criticism, our loyalty always stronger than our discouragement, our faith always stronger than our difficulties. "Charity is patient, is kind, feels no envy, has no selfish aims, cannot be provoked, does not brood over injury, rejoices at the victory of truth; charity hopes ALL things." Lord, present in your holy Church among us, to whom else should we go?

Passiontide

20 | Divine Paradox

The element of paradox is one of the most striking aspects of the Christian religion. In the meeting of the human and the divine, the finite and the infinite, it is inevitable that there should appear a kind of contradiction. For in this our faculties are trying to grasp what is beyond all human comprehension. Our mind, in striving to define God, who is reality itself, essential being, is reduced to saying constantly what God is not, defining by negation that which is most purely positive. And our will, created to find all its joy in loving the infinite good, yet only manages it through sacrifice. It is not, of course, that the contradiction is in God, who is, in the deepest sense, infinitely simple; the paradox arises in us. Our complex mind, faced with the radiance of the infinite, has to approach the infinite by one fractional angle at a time; then, realizing the inadequacy of this, it has to back away again, as it were, to qualify, complement, and harmonize apparent contradictions. The narrow lens of our intellect can only focus on one aspect of infinite truth at a time; and we are always having to refocus, to correct the distortions.

But as well as this inevitable paradox, arising from the very nature of things, there is also what we might almost call a deliberately chosen paradox in the relation between God and man. First, there is the supreme paradox, freely and wonderfully willed by God, of the Incarnation itself: the man who was God, the God who was man. But following upon that great initial fact, there is the whole paradoxical *way* of Jesus, the way of the cross, the sign of contradiction. And the whole Christian life, the way of those who strive to follow Christ, is therefore full of this element of paradox, this dying that we may live. This does not always strike and astonish us, because we have become accustomed to expect and to recognize as almost normal this strange way of the spiritual life. But it is only because Christ has shown us this way, his way, that we begin to recognize it; it is otherwise utterly unimaginable to nature and to the world.

And it is not surprising that at the heart of the Christian mystery we find the paradox set forth most strikingly of all. Holy Week opens with the blessing of palm branches, the procession, the hosannas, commemorating our Savior's triumphant entry into Jerusalem. It must have looked, on the first Palm Sunday, as though his success was assured, the glory of his kingdom at hand. Yet in a few days, while those same branches of palm and olive, symbols of victory and peace, still lay in the dust of the road, he was being led to crucifixion. And perhaps that brief triumph of Palm Sunday was accepted, not so much as a bid for popular leadership, but as a gentle satire on worldly success, contrasting that brief worldly triumph and popularity with the contempt and loneliness in which he was to die.

The account of the entry into Jerusalem, in St. John's Gospel, is followed by the incident of the Greeks who came to the Apostle Philip, seeking an interview with our Lord. Again, this would seem to be a sign of success: the fame and message of Christ were to be carried beyond the limits of his own land. Yet our Lord replies with one of his most memorable, and at the same time most paradoxical, utterances:

"The hour is come for the Son of Man to be glorified. Amen, Amen, I say unto you, unless the grain of wheat fall into the ground and die, itself remains alone. But if it die, it brings forth much fruit. He that loves his life shall lose it, and he that hates his life in this world keeps it unto life eternal."

And if these words are too difficult for men to understand, the same truth will be shown forth also in deeds. The greatest example, the greatest proof, of this life-giving death, this fruitful burial, is to follow quickly, with our Lord's own death on the cross, and then his glorious resurrection. This was the death that was to destroy death, this the burial that raises to newness of life.

But before Calvary there was to be given another demonstration of this paradox of life and death. If the sacrifice of Christ on the cross was the greatest act of divine love for men, his mystical death in the eucharistic sacrifice of the Last Supper was to be the greatest showing forth of that love through the centuries. The institution of the Blessed Eucharist, the bread of life, is intimately connected with the sacrificial death of Christ. The body is broken and offered, that it may be our spiritual food; the blood is poured out, that it may be our spiritual drink. "Take and eat; this is my body which is given for you . . . This is the chalice, the new testament in my blood, shed for you."

The paradox is reflected in the liturgy of Holy Thursday, with its twofold character of joy and sadness. Joy, because we are celebrating the institution of the Blessed Eucharist, with all that that means to the Church. "The right hand of the Lord has wrought strength; the right hand of the Lord has exalted me; I shall not die, but live, and declare the works of the Lord"—this is the triumphant, grateful, Offertory Verse. And think of the exultant *Pange lingua* sung during the procession to the altar of repose. Yet the joy of Holy Thursday is the joy of holy love, not merely jubilant, but deeply tender, mingled with sorrow and sadness. For as she celebrates and rejoices in her great gift, the Church is conscious also of the price her Lord pays in giving this gift of himself—the price of his death upon the cross. And so she sings also, in the Introit: "But it behooves us to glory in the cross of our Lord Jesus Christ; in whom is our salvation, life and resurrection." She remembers, too, that this was the price of our sin; and she prays with special solemnity, humility, and hope, in the Collect: "O God, from whom Judas received the punishment of his guilt, and the thief the reward of his confession, grant us the fruit of your clemency; that as our Lord Jesus Christ in his passion gave recompense to each according to his merits, so he may deliver us from our old sins, and bestow on us the grace of his resurrection."

Well, it is not hard, in theory at least, to apply these great paradoxes of our redemption to our own lowly lives, to our own poor souls which have to be saved and sanctified in this same way: the dying daily to ourselves, in order to live more and more to God; the detachment from all things, that we may possess the treasures of God; the abandonment of our will, that it may find the fullness of love; the descent of humility, that we may be raised to union with God. The theory of all this is very familiar; the practice of it will always remain very hard, and often, all we may be able to do is to stumble on in faith and patience. But Easter is the feast of light and life; amongst its many graces, may our Savior grant us the light of an ever-deepening faith, a life that belongs ever more and more to him. So that that final wonderful paradox may come true: "I live now, not I, but Christ lives in me."

21 | Blessed Mystery of Sorrow and Joy

Every day of our life is a day of grace; every day brings us the invitation to share in the redemptive work of Christ; every day the body of Christ is sacramentally broken for us and the blood of Christ shed for us to be our strength and our refreshment as we follow him. But the holy season of Passiontide is a very special time of grace and sacrifice and eucharistic renewal. The whole year until now has been a preparation for this, and all that follows is the development and flowering of this mystery. The Savior has swiftly run his course on our earth, and his hour has come—the hour which is the climax and fulfillment of his divine mission. And this fulfillment is found to be the paschal mystery. It is a sorrowful mystery because it is fulfilled through the cross, the great price of our redemption; but it is a joyful mystery because it is the perfect oblation of divine love; and it is a triumphant mystery because his resurrection is the source of all our newness of life.

The Church never speaks of the bitter passion of Christ, but always of the blessed passion of Christ. We should indeed meditate with compassion and compunction on the suffering of our Lord, but we should find in it the supreme sign of his love for us and the great example of suffering turned to holiness and love. Every Mass is given to us as a memorial of

Christ's passion: "Do this in remembrance of me"—the remembrance of divine love, of redemptive suffering. And every Mass is an invitation to each of us to unite our suffering with his, to share his redemptive oblation: "Let this mind be in you which was in Christ Jesus." The daily sacramental sharing in Christ's oblation through the Mass calls for a new attitude in the Christian mind and heart. In place of the proud and selfish reactions of natural and worldly instincts, we are invited to the supernatural responses of patience, humility, generosity, trust, and love; that is, we are to live by faith. Only the constant remembrance of the suffering and love of Christ, enlivened by the sacramental power of his living body and blood in the Eucharist, can enlighten our mind and enkindle our will enough to achieve this response. But suffering accepted in that spirit will sanctify, purify, and intensify our true Christian life, and lead us swiftly to divine love.

It may be helpful to recall that the word "sacrifice" is not of itself essentially concerned with pain and suffering. It is derived from the Latin *sacrum facere,* meaning to make holy, that is, to devote to God. In itself this is one of the deepest and truest instincts in the human heart and in all creation. Nothing really exists for itself alone; everything reaches out toward others and ultimately to God. It is a fundamental and inescapable instinct of the mind and heart of man to turn from himself to his Creator. In this his holiness and happiness are rightly found, just as in turning to himself in selfishness he finds at last only sin and unhappiness. But the trouble is that our fallen state of sin, or at least the effect of sin, is already in possession; and it no longer comes easily or naturally to us to turn from ourselves to God, our true end. That is why in this life our turning to God often involves conflict and some kind of suffering for us, why our service of worship and obedience and praise is also a sacrifice which our blessed Lord himself warned us is like dying daily.

Indeed, the great task of restoring true order in a creation disordered by sin was totally beyond mankind's own powers; but the infinite mercy of God found the way of the Incarnation to restore all things in Christ. By him, essentially the great work of atonement is done; yet its redemptive grace has to reach every soul born into this world. And this is made possible because we are not only born into this world but born again in Christ by water and the Holy Spirit, that is, by baptism and the grace of faith. In this way we are truly incorporated, embodied, in Christ; we are not on our own, and our Christian life is not only ours but his also: "I live now, not I, but Christ lives in me." Therefore, by his power and by his holiness, our sharing in his sacrifice can truly be achieved; and our humble sacrifice ceases to be poor and unworthy, for it is made acceptable by the perfect oblation of Christ himself. When we try to follow him in spirit and in truth, we can say, "With Christ I am nailed to the cross." Each Mass is given to us as the sign of this oblation and as the means of sacramental grace enabling us to offer ourselves more and more truly. In the Mass the water and wine of our ordinary life of faith and sacrifice are consecrated and transformed into a holy service, a holy sharing in the passion of Christ, a pledge of sharing in his glory.

22 | The True Light

The theme of light is strikingly used by the Church to sym-
bolize the Savior himself, the eternal truth he makes known
to us, and the kindling of our soul by grace, by which we
accept his teaching and himself.

The first rays came on the very first day of Advent: "Behold the Lord shall come . . . and there shall be in that day a
great light, alleluia." All during Advent the light grew, and
just before Christmas the dawn was greeted with the great *O
Oriens*: "O Rising Sun, splendor of eternal light, sun of justice, come and enlighten those who sit in darkness and the
shadow of death." And then he came, in the sweet hiddenness
of Bethlehem, to those whose pure and simple gaze was ready
for the mystery: "O God, you have made this most holy night
shine forth with the brightness of true light . . . grant that we
may enjoy his happiness in heaven, the mystery of whose
light we have known on earth . . ." Then came the full blaze
of the Epiphany, the manifestation of the Messiah to the
whole world: "Arise, be enlightened Jerusalem, for your
light is come—the Gentiles shall walk in your light, and kings
in the brightness of your rising." And all during the weeks
following the Epiphany, his light shines forth; the Sunday
Gospels bring us the Messiah calling men to the true light,
teaching by his parables, witnessing by his miracles, inviting
by his love. And the voice and heart of the Church, that is, of

those who receive and welcome him, are lifted up to him, recognizing with joy the great works of the Savior as he comes to fulfill his divine mission, to establish his kingdom. Then, with the arrival of Septuagesima, the great light is obscured and darkened by the shadow cast by the guilt of sin. From the first bright revelation of divine love, our gaze turns back for a time to the ashes of our fallen mortality, in which, by prayer and fasting, the divine vocation is to be still worked out. For after the darkness of Lent and Passiontide, the divine light will shine out more wonderfully and clearly than ever, in the resurrection of Christ, and we shall sing "light of Christ" on the night which is all light.

"In your light, we shall see the light . . ." What is the supreme truth, the one supreme light, which the light of grace, the light of Christ, shows to us? The light of the Gospels reveals to us Jesus Christ, God made man. But what is it that the Incarnation itself reveals to us? It is the most simply stated but most wonderful truth of all: God loves us. God loves us with an infinite love; that is the supreme truth. In that light, all else is seen and believed; without that light, nothing else has light for sinful creatures; there is no faith, no hope, without the light shining from the infinite love of God.

Once our faith is given to this stupendous fact of God's love, the great things that follow can be accepted in joyful simplicity, in humble trust, in the spirit of our Lady's *Magnificat*. For the knowledge that we are loved by God is greater than the thought of all the great things he works in us. But, just as on God's side, from that one sublime love of his, there flow forth many different acts—the sending of his Son for our redemption, our regeneration into supernatural life through his Church, the countless daily graces to each one of us—so,

on our side, from the one essential heart of religion, our love
of God, there must flow forth many different acts. The acts
that come from God have a divine magnificence about them,
while the acts that come from us have the lowliness insepara-
ble from our state as creatures and sinners. But even the
humblest act of ours can and must finally spring from love;
and if it does, then it is transformed, and reflects some of the
sublimity of God's own love and God's own acts.

Perhaps this is the reason why we find a twofold element
always in the Church's prayer. There is, on the one hand,
what we might call the mystic, dogmatic, or contemplative
side, in which we contemplate the light of God's love for man
and express the love of our soul for God in great lyrical
elevations of the mind and heart. And, on the other hand,
there is what we might call the moral or didactic side, as
expressed, for instance, in the Epistles and Gospels. This concerns the necessary consequences, the effects and manifestations, of the true love of God in the *acts* of our lives. Now the
Church has many different things to teach us concerning the
manner of life arising from love of God, but time and time
again throughout the year we are led to see this in the setting
of fraternal charity, love of our neighbor: "The man that
loves his neighbor has done all that the law demands."

But you cannot really love your neighbor in general,
merely as an abstract idea. That can so easily be just talk,
high sounding but escaping the real calls of charity close at
hand. Truly, charity begins at home. Of course we must be
ready to act kindly to all men, ready to love all; but to be true
and real, charity must come down to cases. It does not really
start by grandiose projects for the good of all; it starts by
exercising true charity, by showing real love, toward our
friends and family, toward those immediately around us,

those to whom we are intimately bound. Wider works of charity can only safely grow out of the true love practiced toward the people living close to us—love follows knowledge. Furthermore, charity, besides being a great supernatural gift, is in part a habit and, therefore, must be developed through actual practice. It is a dubious kind of charity that finds all its satisfaction in ambitious projects and is left with neither interest nor tenderness nor time for those at home.

One of the great graces (as well as one of the great trials) of family life, of common life, is precisely that it does offer so much opportunity, almost so much compulsion, to practice charity. This applies in religious community life, and it certainly holds true for ordinary Christian family life. The psalmist sings, "See how good and joyful it is for brethren to dwell together in unity." To practice this kind of charity is very difficult, because our nature, even in the best of men, craves, or at least enjoys, independence, freedom, space, peace. But this is really the great opportunity, precisely this state of fraternal dependence. For think, first, how fatally easy it is, in conditions of complete independence, for men to become entirely selfish. A rich bachelor, for example, without family ties or responsibilities, where few demands are made on his patience or humility, who is able to travel about, to follow the latest notion, is not getting much help toward the practice of love, of charity. Rather, everything is tending to the exact opposite: selfishness.

On the other hand, although the effect is unfortunately not automatic or infallible, the state most favorable to the development of unselfishness and charity is the state of those who, while different in personality, taste, and opinions, share a common life and a degree of mutual dependence. In this state, if we are really trying to fulfill the duties of our vocation, we are almost *compelled* to accommodate ourselves to others, to make our wishes and ideas and activities not independent, but in the right sense dependent on one another, not self-centered, but centered on others and through them on God. This is the very nature of life together and, in a way, its very purpose. Whether the result will be a state of penitential frustration for us or whether it will be "good and joyful" will depend a good deal on the dispositions with which we learn to face this life day by day. Certainly it will always be in some way a state of self-denial, and difficult to our nature; but it can also be, simultaneously, good and joyful, as the love of God grows in us.

Now not everyone is living a full community life in a monastery or in matrimony; and for some people the state of loneliness plays a larger part among the instruments of their oblation—this, too, has its own special graces. But all are members of the one mystical body of Christ; all in fact do have a degree of community life through religious, social, and even business activities. So for all of us, as St. Paul says, charity is the bond which makes us perfect. And it will always be in the light and warmth of charity that the light of Christ will be seen among men.

During the period of Lent the revelation of the brightness of the eternal Word is eclipsed in the humility and suffering of his humanity. But on Calvary, while the created sun is obscured, the fire of divine love blazes forth; and then on Easter night the tender radiance of the light of Christ returns to enlighten our souls more than ever. During Lent we try, by prayer and fasting, but especially by growth in true charity, to prepare our souls for that light. We try to turn from our sins, because God is love, because he loves us with an infinite love. That is the true light.

23 | It Is Consummated

The age in which we live, the age which we have to redeem as well as find in it our own salvation, is an age of extremes. On the one hand, we stand at every moment in the shadow of total destruction; on the other, we journey unceasingly toward totally new achievements. We have crossed the threshold of the conquest of space; we have attained control of many diseases; we have even, so we think, reached a deeper understanding of man himself. And yet, more painfully perhaps than in any other age, so many people, especially young people, find it an age of uncertainty, confusion, purposelessness.

Human history seems, in fact, to blunder from one crisis to another, to survive one war only to shudder on the verge of a worse one. On the merely natural and rational level, mankind is tempted to pessimism, tempted to philosophies of meaninglessness, existentialism, relativity, and despair. But suddenly, in a unique moment of human history, we hear the words "It is consummated." These words are uttered on, of all the days in history, the first Good Friday—the day that would seem to be the day of greatest failure, of most tragic frustration. And yet, "It is consummated." There is at last perfect achievement, perfect fulfillment; meaning is given to history, significance to all the suffering, hope to all the failures. It is in this achievement that we set our faith; it is in this consummation that we find our hope.

If Christ was able to say it is achieved, it was because from his cross he was not gazing at worldly values, but eternal ones. He was looking at the holy will of the Father, at the mission he had been sent to fulfill, and at his own consummation of this work. In his own perfect oblation he saw his mission victoriously achieved for the redemption of mankind; and he saw the whole history of mankind take a totally different direction from that moment. On Calvary he could truly say, "Father, I have finished the work thou gavest me . . . it is consummated." It was the achievement possible and intelligible only in total love, that totality of love which is the mystery of God himself. "Greater love than this no man has . . ."

And if there remains always the mystery of the cross and the problem of pain, Christ's pain and ours, may we not answer this difficulty, at least in some part, on the very basis of the realism and existentialism of the philosophers of this world? Could we really imagine Christ as a "success" in this world? Can we think of him dying peacefully in honored old age? No, he came to share the common fate of man, to live our life as it really is in this world. So he shared our failure, our suffering, our sometimes cruel death. The Son of God was so truly and fully Son of Man that he himself could ask his disciples, "Did it not behoove the Christ to suffer . . . and so enter into his glory?"

Could our faith really ask anything other than this for its basis? Yet, of course, our Christian life remains a tremendous act of faith and hope. We accept with grateful joy this great central act of achievement, this one saving consummation of life and death in which all things are renewed, gathered up, and ordained to heavenly life; but our acceptance is precisely in the great grace and act of Christian faith. That faith is the urce of all our Christian life; without that faith everything se in our religion would be empty ceremony.

The newness of life which is the joyful message of Christ's esurrection does not really just mean that certain aspects of ur life must now be different, that there must be a better egulation of our behavior. It means exactly what it says—it is new life, a whole new way of existing. Our human nature as created by God from the beginning in such a way that it ould be taken up into the life of God himself. This was ealized in a perfect and unique way in the Incarnation, hen an individual human nature was taken into personal nion with the eternal Word. But it is the sublime vocation nd destiny of all of us now, through our union with Christ n baptism, faith, and love, to share in his divine sonship and fe—"By whom he has given us great promises, by which we nay be made partakers of the divine nature." Through the ife, death, and resurrection of Jesus Christ, we already begin o see what it means to be a man, even though now "we see as n a glass darkly"; but when the heavenly Easter light shines n us, we shall understand at last what God, in the plenitude f infinite love, means us to be for all eternity.

That is the faith we confess; that is the life to which we ledicate ourselves by our baptismal vows. I believe in Jesus Christ our Lord, who for us men and our salvation was born f the Virgin Mary, suffered, died, and rose again. Alleluia.

Easter

24 | Light of Christ

As we keep vigil on Easter eve for the resurrection of Christ, as the paschal candle's blessed new light dispels the darkness, we are summoned to renew our baptismal promises and solemnly affirm our Christian faith. And surely that is the spontaneous and ardent response of the Christian heart as the light of Christ awakens it. How great is the gift of faith! How clearly the light of Christ makes divine truth known to us, far more surely than any mere human experience. The disciples of Christ saw all the great drama of the passion, death, and resurrection pass before their very eyes; and yet so often holy scripture has to record that "they understood not" and "some doubted." Only by the Pentecostal gift of faith did they recognize the truth which made them free. For faith is the communication of Christ's own Spirit, the sharing in his own divine knowledge, that true knowing of the Father which is eternal life. Therefore we renew the baptismal consecration, which incorporates us in Christ, and we joyfully confess our Christian faith; for by baptism and faith we are born again of water and the Holy Spirit, and live to God.

It is important to notice how concrete, how uncompromising, our profession of faith is: "I believe in one Lord Jesus Christ . . . Who for us men and for our salvation came down from heaven and became flesh by the Holy Spirit of the Virgin Mary: and was made man. He was also crucified for us, suffered under Pontius Pilate, and was buried. And on the third day he rose again according to the scriptures . . . I believe in the resurrection of the body and life everlasting." Life everlasting was achieved for us by the one mediator Jesus Christ, true God and true man, who came to our earth for this purpose alone. It was by the perfect oblation of his human life, body and soul, heart and mind, that he saved us—by everything that we ourselves would mean by our personal human life. In all his human reality, including the final decisive act of death itself, as all this was made infinitely holy because he was also true God, he won our salvation. It was for this that he took the reality of our flesh, so that his divine life could truly come to us.

And it is in his flesh, and ours, that we are to work out our Christian vocation, in the truth and reality of our personal human life as it is illumined by the light of faith and directed by supernatural love. There is no other way to do it; no mere theory, no abstract ideal, will serve. It is easy to enunciate ideals, but we live on the level of realities. Our Christian life is not fulfilled on the level of attractive theories; that would be easy, but empty. It must be fulfilled in facts, in living.

So what we celebrated at Christmas was not an idea, but a fact: the birth in our flesh of Jesus Christ, born of a woman. It was not just a prophetic sign, not just a proclamation of a beautiful law of love, not just a word revealed; it was the Word Incarnate. The good news at Christmas was very specific: the Savior is born in our flesh. And, likewise at Easter, we confess that same human flesh of Christ risen from the dead: not a spirit, not a symbol, but a living man whose body carried the scars of his wounds to be seen and touched. And now, in that body of Christ risen in the freedom of divine life, the grace of his Holy Spirit is made wonderfully communicable to all our race. That is why we go on to say in our creed: "I believe in the holy Catholic Church." Our Christian vocation is accomplished through our actual faith and life in the body of Christ now living and acting among men in his poor, sinful, holy, wonderful Church on earth.

Men have always been tempted to turn away from the concrete reality, from the imperfect body, to seek the purely "spiritual," away from the disappointing and scandalous blemishes of the institution to the perfection of pure love, brotherhood, enlightenment. But that is to turn away, finally, from reality, from people. Christian faith, the gospel of the Incarnation, holds that our salvation is in the Man-God who was born and suffered and died and rose again in his human flesh. And now he lives with us and in us still, as he promised, as a body, as a Church embodied in men, to continue his saving work of teaching and sanctifying. In that Church, living, imperfect, as members of his one body, and in our own living, imperfect humanity, we seek and find his grace and love, our sacrifice and salvation, our death and resurrection.

Christ's baptism in the Jordan by John was a sign and beginning of his whole mission as redeemer and servant, as Lamb of God who by his perfect oblation would take away the sins of the world. And that first baptism would find its fulfillment in his baptism of blood, his blessed passion and death. For he himself said, as he approached his hour, the hour of our redemption: "I have a baptism with which I must be baptized; and how I am constrained until it is accomplished." Our own baptism into Christ and his body, his Church, is also the beginning of a mission: our vocation to Christian life and death in Christ, a life of faith, a gradual conversion of our whole heart to that loving obedience to the

Father of which Christ gave us the perfect example. And so we are made ready for the baptism of Christian death which is our final communion with Christ's death and resurrection. By his merciful grace, at that blessed moment our eyes will open in full recognition at last, and as Christian faith passes into heavenly vision, we shall cry out the same beautiful words of our paschal vigil, but then how joyfully, gloriously: "Light of Christ! Thanks be to God! Alleluia!"

25 | I Know That My Redeemer Lives

"I know that my Redeemer lives." These words, recorded in the Book of Job, were written long ago, long before our Redeemer entered into our time. Yet, with that strange force characteristic of prophecy, which knows no past or future, they go to the very heart of our Christian faith. My Redeemer lives; this is the source of all the rest; without this there is nothing. If Christ is not risen, all our faith is in vain and we are the most wretched of men. But if he is risen, then he is the firstfruits of the dead, the resurrection and the life, the beginning and the end, the fountain of everlasting life for all creation.

Somehow, too, these same words utter the deepest instinct of each individual Christian soul. I may be personally troubled and confused by many aspects of life, even about many aspects of my faith; and yet through it all and perhaps despite it all, "I know that my Redeemer lives," and my hope and my faith stand firm.

Our life on this earth is always going to be a rather strange and difficult, but wonderful, combination of Passiontide and Eastertide. The liturgical seasons themselves reflect this mixture and are not so categorical as we perhaps think; in this, too, we are offered guidance for our daily life. For instance, in Passiontide the Church tries to keep step almost hour by hour with her Savior in the events of his sacred passion and death, and she sorrows both for his sufferings and for our sins which have caused them. But the Church can never really forget that in fact Christ's victory is won, salvation is promised, grace is everywhere, even in suffering and trouble, so even in Passiontide the Eucharist is celebrated for our salvation in thanksgiving, peace, and joy. But then we must acknowledge also the other side. In this life, even when we have in our Christian faith so much reason for hope and joy, yet we are never really far from sadness. We walk in the shadow of our mortality and weakness; and we remain only too vulnerable to the effects of evil in a creation so deeply disordered by sin that the work of grace will not be completed until the last moment of time. In our frailty we are often troubled by fear, doubt, and guilt; many things seem to go wrong, in our prayer, our work, our plans, our vocation, our personal life. Yet, somehow, by the ultimate and strongest grace of our faith, we can still say, "I know my Redeemer lives"; and nothing else really matters.

It is at times a great relief to try to forget ourselves and to let our joy center unselfishly in our Redeemer, to rejoice only in the boundless and unimaginable joy of the risen Christ. We know that we are quite safe in thus forgetting ourselves, for we know well that he never forgets us. In his last beautiful and touching prayer before he left his disciples, our Savior prayed: "This, Father, is my desire, that all those whom you have entrusted to me may be with me where I am." It is as though he is saying that heaven will not be heaven for him unless we are there. This is a beautiful manifestation of the sublime mystery of God's creative love. Somehow, wonderfully, the only one who could have truly forgotten all else, the only one who was truly perfect and complete in his own being, one but not alone in the blessed richness of the Trinity—this One willed not to be without us; this One called us into existence and into his loving friendship.

The bond of creature and Creator is already in itself a relationship far more intimate and personal than any bond of parental relationship known to us. But then this relationship was made infinitely more close and loving when God took our humanity to himself in a personal substantial union in Jesus Christ and, through that sacred humanity, communicated divine life to each one of us baptized in him. He has called each one of us to himself by name, by his creative personal intimate knowledge and love: "I have loved you with an everlasting love; therefore I have drawn you to my heart, having pity on you."

Of all the virtues, it seems to me that hope is the easiest to practice. So long as God is, and is what he is, we can trust most peacefully in his loving care of us. From any other friend, however good and generous, we know that we can expect only limited attention and care. But the wonderful thing about God is that his wisdom and love are never divided or distracted. We can always count in a most literal and perfect sense upon God's "undivided attention." "He loved me and gave himself for *me* . . ." Each one of us can always say in the utter confidence of supernatural hope: "I know that my Redeemer lives."

26 | It Is the Lord

"You seek Jesus of Nazareth who was crucified; he is risen, he is not here." Must we not do a kind of spiritual double take at this Easter message of the angel? The force of it suddenly hits us: he is *not* here. What is the angel saying? Did we not expect the words: he is risen, he is here, everything is all right, everything is going to go on as before? No, that was the lesson the disciples took so long to learn, the lesson that we have still to learn. He lives now in newness of life, by heavenly life not earthly life. He will indeed abide with us until the end of time, but by his Spirit among us and in us, by his Church and his sacraments, by the life of faith. This is to be his victory and our victory, the victory which overcomes the world: our faith. Yet, like his first disciples, we would still have him come to us on our terms, to deal with us in ways acceptable to us. How often do we echo St. Thomas, "Unless I touch and see his human mortality, I will not believe," or the holy women to whom he had to say gently, "Do not cling to me so." To these, and to us, he had to teach the life of faith: "It is better for you that I go."

Our Christian life is always to be a life of faith. Sometimes after we have been talking or reading about the great ideals and principles of religion, we come down to the level of our own personal life with a feeling of inadequacy and discouragement. There always seems to be such a gap between the theory, the ideal, and the living human individual case, not only a gap in the sense of achievement but also in the sense of applicability, procedure, contact, security. But it is precisely this gap which is the opportunity, the challenge, the grace. It is the invitation to launch out into the deep. We do not and cannot live on the level of theories, of ideals; we live on the level of daily human reality, the concrete case. But somehow this daily reality of our life has to be enacted in the light of God's eternal purposes, that is, it has to be lived in faith, in trust, and in humble love. Our Lord did not promise to those who would follow him a life of special knowledge and power. When that overzealous mother asked that her sons should sit one at his right hand and one at his left hand in the kingdom, he replied that this was not his to give, and he could promise only: "My chalice indeed you shall drink." He offered a share in his sacrifice and oblation, in all its mystery, in all its faith and love.

Since the victory of Christ's redemptive sacrifice, the world indeed *is* now "saved," all *is* now "grace." That is, all is now susceptible of goodness; all is now the material of our sanctification; the power of evil is indeed broken. Yet some of the sad deep effects of sinfulness remain; there is a kind of awkwardness, and heaviness, and darkness in all that material which is somehow to be turned to our sanctification. All things do indeed work together for good, but not without difficulty and anxiety. When our Lord returned in his risen person to his disciples, they seemed to have difficulty even in recognizing him. They had to reassure each other that "it is the Lord" or recognize him by some special sign, in the breaking of bread. This will often be our task and our grace, to recognize and give our faith and our obedience and love to the Lord when he comes to us in all the events of our daily life, in our work, our joy, our suffering, our families, our friends, the sick, the poor; we have to tell ourselves, "It is the Lord."

The truth and wisdom of God, the holy will of God, hardly ever come to us in such visible, tangible manner as to "satisfy" our human ideas and preferences. In different ways and in different degrees, our faith and trust will always be needed. It is part of the oblation of man's gift of himself to God. It demands supernatural courage and even a kind of spiritual optimism, as well as the humility and self-surrender of our Lady's "Be it done unto me according to your word." Our risen Savior, when he accepted Thomas' conditions in the upper room and allowed him to touch the sacred wounds, did at the same time rebuke him, however tenderly, however patiently, for his lack of faith. "Because you have seen, you have learned to believe." Somehow, our Lord is saying, somehow you should have known, somehow you should have trusted: "Blessed are they who have not seen and have believed."

For we are not now dealing with rational processes of the mind inquiring about the existence of a supreme being; we are not weighing the arguments, following the laborious chain of reasoning to the threshold of faith. We *have* now, by God's mercy, that first great gift of faith. We are dealing with the Lord we know, the Lord who has come to us, who has entered into a personal relationship with us. It is this Lord who asks our faith and trust: "Be not faithless but believing." It is this Lord who warns us that there will be difficulties such as might deceive even the elect, yet who asks us to stand fast in our faith in him, in our hope and trust and obedience and love, sharing his chalice as well as as his friendship, because "it is the Lord."

27 | Cause for Joy

At the Offertory of the Mass on Low Sunday we pray: "Receive, we beseech you, O Lord, the gifts of your exultant Church; and grant that she to whom you have given cause for so great joy, may obtain also the fruit of perpetual gladness."

There are two main themes which make the Church's joy overflow so beautifully during the octave of Easter. First, of course, is the contemplation of the risen Savior: "This is the day which the Lord has made, let us rejoice and be glad in it." But secondly, notwithstanding her eager desire to contemplate the glory of her risen Lord, the Church manages to keep a very attentive maternal eye on her new children, those who, at least during the early centuries and again in our own time, are baptized during the Easter vigil and first receive the body of their Lord at the Easter Mass. For these too are a great cause of joy to the Church, these who are born to her of water and the Holy Spirit, as the firstfruits of her Lord's sacrifice in the "victory which overcomes the world, our faith."

Perhaps it is well to admit though, when we begin to speak of the great joy of these days, that we cannot all individually pretend to be experiencing floods of joy. We taste some joy, we hope, and yet we may be only too conscious that we are far from really filling our souls from the fountains of spiritual joy which spring forth at Christ's resurrection. This is due to various causes, some of them our own responsibility and some of them beyond our control. It may be that the feast is in part spoiled for us by the fact that we are still very worldly, distracted in mind and will, not really spiritual enough to give ourselves wholly to spiritual joys or for them to be given to us. Then, besides this possibility, there are all those contingencies beyond our own control, which remind us that we are living on earth, not in heaven, in time, not in eternity: illness, anxieties, family and business problems. Such cannot help but limit even the joys of the spirit.

Yet, despite all this, it remains true that Eastertide is a time of special joy. As the years go by, and as Easter comes to us anew each year, we hope that we may share its joy more deeply, truly, spiritually. Meanwhile we can at any rate sing a humble "Thanks be to God" for the joy of the Church, for the joy of God himself. "And they shall sing in the ways of the Lord, for great is the glory of the Lord." As the newly blessed paschal candle cast its holy light into the darkened church at the Easter vigil, the deacon's triumphal call was heard, "The light of Christ"; and we all sang, "Thanks be to God." And as the light of Christ advanced through the Church, and spread to priest and to people, we were unable to restrain that exultant, mounting cry: "The light of Christ —Thanks be to God." And when the whole church was filled with the new light of Christ, the deacon broke into one of the most lyrical chants of the whole year: "Now let the heavenly hosts rejoice." This paschal hymn is filled with the loving boldness of holy joy: "How inestimable is your love, that you have delivered up your Son to redeem your slave: oh happy fault of Adam which was to have such a Redeemer!" Before the vigil was ended, the paschal alleluia was solemnly in-toned, and then taken up by all the church; and this alleluia will run its silver thread through all the varying joyful modu-lations of the whole Easter liturgy.

As to the other subject of the Church's thought and prayer during these days, namely her new children, well, children are always a source of both joy and solicitude, and so we find the heart of the Church both gladdened by the heavenly increase granted to her by the waters of baptism and, at the same time, full of care and anxiety for her children's future. She well knows that the first fervor and joy must pass, that there awaits those who now feel that nothing can ever take away their happiness and peace the long probation of all the temptations and weariness of their earthly pilgrimage. And so the liturgy is also full of instruction and exhortation for the newly baptized and of earnest prayer for their faithful perseverance.

And the renewal of our baptismal vows, at the Easter vigil, reminds each one of us of the great grace of spiritual rebirth which has been ours and of our unceasing holy duty to strive to walk always in that newness of life. Conscious as we must be of our many stumblings and hesitations, it is yet some consolation to us to know that by our renewal and rededication we have wished to show our Lord our good will to fulfill and to perfect that first consecration of our baptism. We may not have succeeded very well, but at least we should be humbly grateful that we have been given by God's grace some inkling of supernatural wisdom, some spark of divine love, to help us decide to try to live faithfully in the light of Christ. May his grace make up for the failures of our frail nature; and may we make our own the Collect which closes the Easter octave: "Grant us, we beseech you, almighty God, that we who have celebrated the paschal festival may, through your bounty, ever cleave to its spirit in our conversion of life."

28 | Alleluia from Head to Foot

There is a lovely saying of St. Augustine: "The Christian should be an alleluia from head to foot." But one cannot help asking: What about when I am not an alleluia, but an ache, from head to foot; when I am full of anxiety and gloom? Well, the Christian alleluia is not exactly a pain-killer or a tranquilizer, though as a matter of fact we can gratefully recognize that it does indeed help a great deal in both those directions. But our Christian life and its joy, at least in part, are on a different level of life and are a different kind of life from our earthly life. Do not misunderstand me. I do not mean to say that we are to live two separate lives, a lowly human one and a lofty spiritual one. We are one living person, living one personal life, which is somehow to be both truly supernatural and truly human. The fact is, however, that given the fallen nature of man and the disorder caused by sin, the attempt to integrate the divine and the human elements will always fall short on this earth, and it will find its perfect fulfillment only in heaven.

The prayers and thought of the Church during the paschal season are filled with the paradoxical character of our Christian life. On the one hand, she invites us to "shout for joy to God all the earth, alleluia; sing praise to his great name, alleluia" (Introit, Third Sunday after Easter). On the other hand, in the Gospel of the same Mass, she reminds us of the words of our blessed Lord himself to his disciples: "You will weep and lament, while the world rejoices."

One of the most characteristic elements of the Christian life on earth is precisely this combination of suffering and joy or, rather, this transformation of suffering by faith and hope and love. Christ's saving grace comes to the world as the world really is, finding man in his reality, in the disorder of sin and all the grievous effects of sin. The divine work has to start from there, from reality, not from theory. And the triumph of grace over sin, and of hope and love over suffering, is Christ's true victory and ours: "This is the victory which overcomes the world, our faith." The transformation of evil and the turning of it to good purposes is God's divine prerogative. It is a solemn but true thought that, properly speaking, all that we suffer is really due to our own fault, is the rightful heritage of sin, and is in a terrible sense a foretaste of hell. It is only by Christ's mercy that a complete reversal takes place. By his entering into our world and taking our suffering and guilt upon himself, he enables us to find in suffering the divine instrumentality of redemption which he himself attached to it. We then share his victory over evil, and from being children of darkness and sin we become children of light and holiness; our suffering which had been a foretaste of hell becomes through the touch of his grace a foretaste and gateway of heaven. Our sufferings are, as it were, now consecrated and transformed by the words "Thy will be done," and become occasions of grace instead of occasions of sin, so that in the words of the Apostle Paul we may "glory in tribulation."

So it is not that the Christian life is without suffering; it is, rather, that Christian joy is not in its deepest and truest sense spoiled by suffering. We tend, only too naturally and understandably, to think of happiness as the absence of trouble, and we are always telling each other to forget our troubles. There are indeed times when that is good advice and good practice; but it will not serve all the time, and it comes too close to defining happiness in terms of pleasure rather than joy. I can very clearly remember a well-meaning old priest who used to inquire very solicitously of us boys in school, "Are you happy?" Well, we probably were until that moment, but as soon as we began to worry about it, of course we were not. Christian happiness must be something a good deal maturer and deeper than schoolboy happiness. It is not dependent on the total absence of suffering. Rather, it rises from a firm trust in the transcendent power of God's wisdom and love to make all things, even our troubles, work together finally for our good, our true happiness.

We must not allow ourselves to be too shaken and disturbed by the presence of pains and worries in our lives. This is, I am afraid, the only too normal situation of humanity in a vale of tears. First, we must try to keep the troubles in proper perspective, for even the worst of them will finally pass; secondly, we must try not to allow the troubles to spoil the more joyful elements in our life, as if trouble were *all* we had; and thirdly, we must learn to find even in the troubles themselves that secret but powerful divine element hidden there by Christ himself, which makes them instruments of love and therefore of happiness. So St. Augustine's statement is really true. If we feel that it does not quite fit us, notice exactly what he is saying: "The Christian *should* be an alleluia from head to foot." The *perfect* Christian *will* be an alleluia from head to foot; but we poor, imperfect Christians will be alleluias here and there, with many a groan and lament in between.

The Christian message, even the Easter message, is not so

heartless and false as to pretend there are no problems. But it is always inviting us to lift up our hearts and to find refreshment and hope in the risen Savior. The more we do that, the more we shall become an alleluia. And as to "from head to foot," the last few inches may well have to be filled in as we step over the threshold of heaven, and hear at last with clear and perfect joy the invitation of divine love: "Lift up your hearts."

29 | Sown in Weakness, Rising in Power

As corruption and death entered into God's creation with man's sin, so with the forgiveness of sins we profess our faith in the resurrection of the body. What exactly are we proclaiming in that great statement of faith and hope? Is it some great miracle of divine omnipotence, as yet distant by perhaps thousands of years, when, at the very end of time itself, our bodies will be summoned to rise from dusty death to glorious immortality? Yes, I suppose that is strictly what the dogma states. This very flesh and blood of mine, now so living yet so mortal, so much myself, will be restored, will live again, though in a wholly new transcendent way.

But we can make a much more immediate application of these words: that resurrection which is our Christian newness of life here and now. "You HAVE eternal life," our Lord said to his disciples. The Pasch is the passing of the Christian from death to life, from sin to grace, from the servitude of evil to the freedom of the children of God. And this concerns not just our soul, but our full human person, body and soul.

There is an oversimplified, childish, and even dangerous notion that man is made up of two conflicting parts: the good part, the soul, and the bad part, the body. Within the confines of this notion, the Christian struggle would be to repress the body, ignore it, pretend it is not there, and to try to live as a soul, as an angel. But anybody who has actually tried to follow this procedure has usually found that the man who plays at being an angel soon ends up as a brute, or at least as an ass. We are *not* angels imprisoned in evil bodies; any evil in us is at least as much in our soul as in our body, though our poor body usually gets the blame.

We do experience in our bodies, more vividly perhaps but also more unmistakably, the disorder which sin has left in us: our uncontrolled passions, our fears, our lust, our anger. But our souls also are wounded and disordered, though more subtly and therefore more dangerously, in pride, falsehood, hatred, cowardice, ambition. The "weakness" that is so often our excuse, and which we tend to think of as weakness of the body, is really more often weakness of the soul, of our will, our love, our judgment. Think of the frail bodies of some of the saints, and their great hearts! No, man is really a unique union of soul and body, spirit and matter, one person, one living wonderful work of God, designed to love and glorify God in his own special way, not as an angel, not as a brute, but as a man.

Man is created in God's image and likeness; and if this likeness seems more apparent in our spiritual side, this is surely balanced by the incarnation of the Son of God himself. The eternal Word of the Father took to himself our body and blood, as well as our soul, and made them the instruments of our redemption. It was by his wounds and bruises, as well as by the perfect interior oblation of his soul, that we were saved: "So, on the cross, his own body took the weight of our sins; we were to become dead to our sins, and live for holiness; it was his wounds that healed you." St. Ambrose expresses it: "The Lord Jesus came and did armed service to virtue in the flesh which had been sin's subject. In consequence, our members are no longer weapons of evil but of power." And St. Paul, even more strikingly, says: "Let not sin therefore reign in your mortal body so as to obey the lusts thereof; but present yourselves to God as those that are risen from the dead, and your members as instruments of justice unto God."

Our Christian vocation, therefore, is not to try to live somehow outside our body, against nature, but in our body, as a human being, with all our faculties turned toward God. We cannot go to him, really, except through the human nature in which he himself created us. So it is not a question of destroying, but of fulfilling. "A great price was paid to ransom you; glorify God by making your bodies the shrines of his presence."

But then, what about all the exhortations in Christian spirituality about chastising the body, despising the flesh, and so on? But *of course* these are most true and necessary, rightly understood. They are part of the whole tradition of Christian asceticism, which is only the Greek word for discipline, of body and of soul. Monsignor Knox once wrote of an old lady he heard about who always pronounced the word with the accent on the second syllable: discipline. And he remarks how right she really was, for what we are really talking about is precisely being a disciple of Christ, "discipling," and we cannot follow Christ without discipline, without taking up the cross, without overcoming our disordered instincts.

For we are not, even by the redemptive grace of Christ's risen life which is given to us, yet restored to that perfect integrity and "spirituality" of the body which our first parents possessed and lost, and which we shall enjoy, even more wonderfully, when the full and final effects of the Resurrection and Redemption triumph in our humanity with Christ's final coming in power. Then, in St. Paul's words, "What is sown unhonored rises in glory; what is sown in weakness rises in power; what is sown a natural body rises a spiritual body." But we are not at that stage yet. We are, body and soul, already redeemed at the great price of Christ's own body broken and given for us; we are sealed by his precious blood, a royal priesthood, a kingly people. But we are still burdened with the deep effects of sin, still darkened and wounded in our nature, still weak and subject to temptation.

While we can and must serve God in and through our humanity, in our body as well as our soul, it will continue to be with labor and effort against the disordered instincts of a fallen nature. That is why we speak of taking up the cross, crucifying our passions, making up what is wanting in the sufferings of Christ. And yet this very labor, this very suffering, somehow becomes the supreme instrument of love and holiness and joy. Somehow we have to find the right way to see and employ our humanity and its faculties truly and wholly in the service and love of God, acknowledging our nature's weakness and perilous errors and willfulness, and therefore our need for discipline, humility, and prayer, while yet recognizing the consecrating, sanctifying power of Christ which enables us to resist the evil and to turn all the good in us to God's will, and thus to our own true fulfillment.

Our Christian life on earth is a kind of halfway house: far from the unredeemed guilt and shame of unforgiven sin, but not yet arrived at the perfect glory and spirituality of body and soul in our final resurrection. It is a kind of risen life with Christ on earth, not yet the final ascended life with him in heaven. There, our vocation and our glory will be the surpassing reflection, in us, of the divine splendor we contemplate at last face to face. Here, on earth, the glory is hidden; but thanks to Christ's redemptive grace, it has begun in us already, for it is the vital saving light of faith, the price-less clarity with which we look at this life and earth from the supernatural point of view. That is our risen life, our Easter life on this earth: to live by faith, to rejoice in hope, and to love God with our whole heart, our whole soul, our whole mind, and our whole strength.

Ascension

30 | It Is Expedient to You That I Go

The days between the Ascension and Pentecost have their own special spirit. It seems to be a blending of true joy, because of Christ's triumph, with a kind of wistfulness and expectation. "You men of Galilee, why do you stand looking up to heaven?" This departure of our Lord is a very different one from that by which he was taken from his disciples at the time of his passion. Of that it had been prophesied: "I will strike the shepherd, and the flock shall be dispersed." Then his disciples had been left in grief and terror and darkness. His present going leaves them in joy and hope and peace.

One can in some part understand the joy of our Lady and the disciples, even given the departure of our Lord, if one considers two main reasons. First, the sweetness of his presence was still felt among them; for forty days after his resurrection he had been with them, speaking to them of the kingdom of God; the encouragement of his words, the effect of his presence, would still endure. Then, secondly, their joy would be inspired by his promise of the Paraclete, the Spirit of truth, who would teach them all truth.

And we ourselves, in the life of the Church, really have the same two reasons for joy. Although by the count of the years and the centuries the human presence of Christ is not so recent or vivid to us as it was to the little group on Mount

Olivet and in the Cenacle, yet by the timelessness of the liturgy he remains close to us too. By that touch of eternity which Christ's mystical body enjoys even here on earth, we experience the abiding presence of our Lord, reliving his life with him, sharing in his eucharistic body and blood, so that even though he has ascended into heaven, he is yet always with us.

And secondly, we too have the joy of the promise, that promise so deep in mystery and wonder. "It is expedient to you that I go, for if I go not, the Paraclete will not come to you; but if I go, I will send him to you . . . I have yet many things to say to you, but you cannot bear them now. But when he, the Spirit of truth, is come, he will teach you all truth." How can it possibly be "more expedient" for us that our Lord should depart? Yet Christ himself tells us this, tells us that there are ways in which his Holy Spirit works in us more effectively, more fruitfully, than would the bodily presence of Jesus. This is a striking thought: it is more expedient, it is better for us, to accept the absence of Christ, of all the wonder and power of his visible human presence, of all that his presence meant to his apostles, to whom these words were first addressed, of all that his presence meant to Magdalen and the other holy women, and even of all that his humanity meant to the Mother from whom he had received it. There is mystery here; our mind can hardly conceive how anything could be better for us, more sanctifying, more fruitful, than the visible presence of the sacred humanity of Jesus Christ our Lord.

The significance obviously cannot be to lessen the wonderful blessing and power of the Son of God in his humanity; rather, the significance is that we should realize the blessing and power of Christ through his Holy Spirit. The visible presence of Christ's humanity, this is not for us; but *this* presence, through his Holy Spirit, this is for us. This we are meant to know; this is given to us for our joy and our life; this is "more expedient" for us.

Through his Holy Spirit, Christ comes to us more directly, more closely, more interiorly. Perhaps we can say that Christ assumed our humanity for the purpose of redeeming mankind, and that he sends his Spirit for the purpose of redeeming and sanctifying each individual soul. When he took our human nature upon himself, that he might be one with us and bear the burden of our sin, the Son of God accepted our nature in reality and in truth, with all its creaturely limitations and conditions. He came to win his victory in our lowliness, rather than in his infinity. And this was his way, not only in his conflict with the powers of darkness (as in the temptation, in the crucifixion) but also in his mission to teach and to save men. He did not overwhelm them by infinite power, but drew them after him through his humanity, eliciting their faith and love. He accepted the limitation of communicating the divine message through human language. The depths of the eternal unchanging truth through the shifting shallows of sound that are often inadequate to convey even our own poor thoughts! The WORD, through words! No wonder he said: "I have yet many things to say to you, but you cannot bear them now"—they would be left to the interior teaching of the Spirit whom he would send.

Our Lord accepted, too, the limitations of time and place, within which narrow limits so few men and women heard his divine voice, knew his saving touch. And he accepted death, the leaving of this earth, and the entrusting of his work to others. All these things went with the humanity he so truly took upon himself. Yet the redemptive work could not cease;

therefore, he chose this "more expedient" way in which his mission should go on. It would be in a twofold manner: visibly, through the instrumentality of men, the apostles and their successors; and invisibly, through the interior operation of grace in men's souls. Both of these means are the special work of the Holy Spirit whom Christ promised to send. Both of these instruments, by the wisdom of God, are "more expedient" for us; in both, Christ's redemptive power is applied more effectively to save and to sanctify the individual souls of men through all time.

Yet we know that even the fiery power of the Holy Spirit of Pentecost respects the freedom of men. We know that in a mysterious way the fruit of God's grace does regard man's free acceptance and cooperation: our dispositions of faith, docility, love, are still needed, just as Jesus sought them in the hearts of those he longed to help as he went about doing good. And this applies whether the Holy Spirit works through human representatives or through his interior guidance in our soul. Thus we are exhorted to continued faith, obedience, purity: "Be you doers of the word, and not hearers only."

Because religion is a thing of sincerity and truth, it must indeed always come back to the dispositions of a man's heart. Yet, lest this should seem to throw the whole burden back on our own weak selves again, let us remember how Christ acted while on earth. When our Lord looked for faith, simplicity, love, in the hearts of those he would bless, how generous he was! He did not wait for *perfect* dispositions. "Lord, I do believe; help my unbelief"—this imperfect faith was not rejected. "Grant that these may sit one at your right hand and one at your left, in your kingdom"—this was hardly an ideal motive as a starting point for men who were to be apostles;

yet they were accepted, and learned to drink his chalice in the end. And let us remember the timidity of Nicodemus, the self-assurance of Peter, the jealousies of the twelve apostles. What great works of grace took their start from these imperfect beginnings!

So we too may take courage, confessing our many weaknesses and mixed motives, yet trusting still to the saving, purifying work of the Holy Spirit, the Spirit who is continually about us and within us, offering to us his grace and love day by day. It is helpful to remember that we live, not simply by virtue of some primeval act of creation by God, which made us and left us, but rather by virtue of the ceaseless power of God sustaining us. We exist, from moment to moment, simply because God *wills* us. But God's will is God's love; so it means that we exist moment by moment because God loves us each moment. Ceaselessly he pours forth upon us his creative Spirit of love, not only in the natural order, but still more in the supernatural order to which he has raised us by a new and more wonderful spiritual creation. "Send forth your Spirit, and they shall be created; and you will renew the face of the earth."

Pentecost

31 | Too Good to Be True

A familiar comment on human experience is expressed in the saying "That's too good to be true." It may be said cynically, or resignedly, or even almost cheerfully; but in fact this comment gives sad testimony to the disorder which sin has brought into our world, this world which God himself created and gave to us, and "saw that it was good." Yet now when some aspect of creation, especially some happy possibility in human relations, raises our hope and our heart, we tend to draw back fearfully, telling each other gloomily, "It's too good to be true."

The fact is, of course, that there is basis for this caution. Man has had to learn by painful experience to protect himself against the way things usually turn out. He has learned not to hope for too much in this life, because he has suffered so many painful disappointments. And it seems that, even apart from higher motives of spiritual detachment, we do need to temper with a prudent realism any excessively optimistic expectations about people and things in this world.

Allowing for all this, however, we have to go on to confess with sorrow that this experience of trouble has been allowed to produce the worst effect of all; man has allowed it to turn his own character to cynicism, pessimism, and even despair. All of us suffer from this weakness to some extent. We find it hard to trust in goodness, to let ourselves accept it, even when it is true. No, we say, "That's too good to be true." A certain perversity seems to run through our nature now; sometimes we actually prefer to believe the worse of two alternatives, especially when it concerns our neighbor's character, motives, and probable future. But even about ourselves, we are afraid to hope, to raise up our minds and hearts. How often the Church has to say to us: "Lift up your hearts!" For this discouragement extends to religious and supernatural things, too. Men are tempted to reject the very goodness and truth of God himself. His creative love, his redemptive mercy, his incarnation, his Church and sacraments, his will for our holiness and heavenly life, all this seems too good to be true.

And indeed it is: by the sad experience of fallen, sinful man; by any natural, reasonable standards of created goodness. But that is precisely the point; this is something that we can only begin to understand and believe by divine standards, by the nature and motives of uncreated infinite goodness and love. Of course, it is too good to be true—of us, but not of God.

It would take the Incarnation itself, the personal entry of divine goodness into our world, the coming close of that distant love, to teach man by personal experience the truth of this infinite goodness. Yet, paradoxically, even the Incarnation itself—this above all perhaps—would seem to many "too good to be true." Even the privileged men who saw Christ face to face could not really accept it; our Lord even at the end still had to correct and reprove them: "All this time I have been with you, and still you do not know me, still you do not believe." And again, "I have still many things to tell you, but you cannot bear it, you cannot understand it now." The disciples' attitude toward Christ was still too much of this world, still had too much of worldly wisdom, human experience, in it. And by that standard, of course, Christ's word was incredible, far "too good to be true."

There was needed the last supreme gift, the gift of Christ's own Spirit, that Pentecostal communication of truth and knowledge which we call faith, that sharing in God's own knowing. Then, at last, man knew; man rejoiced to believe and love. How can the wonderful works of God be too good to be true, once they are recognized for what they are? When the Holy Spirit was poured forth upon the disciples in the first Pentecost, they were filled with that Spirit and "began to speak." They proclaimed their faith, their joyful faith that indeed these wonderful works of God were true. They came out of hiding, out of uncertainty and fear, recognizing at last their Lord: the same Lord, yet now in such a different light, such a different Spirit. "This same Jesus whom you crucified . . . God has raised from the dead . . . Salvation is not to be found elsewhere; this alone of all the names under heaven has been appointed to men as the one by which we must be saved."

In the familiar invocation of the Holy Spirit which we make before so many spiritual activities, we pray that we may be "truly wise . . . through Christ our Lord." For wisdom is given to us, not just as words or law, but as a person—a living person who speaks and attracts, who draws even our selfish dull nature to himself. It is true that in this life we must still know him and come to him partly through signs; through his Church, his sacraments, his word in holy scripture, his brethren. Yet now we have within us that living Spirit which enables us to see these signs, to interpret them, and to know and believe in them. He has given to us his Spirit in which we cry Abba, Father, and live in faith and hope and love. In that Spirit we are freed from blindness, from sin and death, from "the law," from "the flesh." In that Spirit his power is made perfect in our weakness. In that Spirit *nothing* is too good to be true!

32 | The Gifts of God

"All things are yours; and you are Christ's; and Christ is God's." This is the good news that Christ the Lord sent the apostles to carry to the ends of the earth: "If God has given us his Son, how has he not in him given us all things?" Indeed, even natural reason has some concept of this condition of man: "According to the almost unanimous opinion of believers and unbelievers alike, all things on earth should be related to man as to their center and crown" (Pastoral Constitution on the Church in the Modern World, Par. 12).

The great gifts of God are not as the little gifts which we make to one another. Our giving is limited, external; we can only give from without. For our possession is never absolute, and so our giving and our receiving always involve a kind of innocent pretense. We even feel a kind of guilt and embarrassment mixed with our pleasure when we receive—"You shouldn't have," we say. We feel that it is a loss to the giver and a somewhat false enrichment of the receiver. For our gifts are mostly things, mostly transitory, perishable tokens— except those intangible gifts which come nearer to reflecting the gifts of God: gifts of friendship, forgiveness, peace, love.

But the gifts of God are not things. They are communications of the living God, the God of life, the God of love; and insomuch as they are *his* gifts, they are in a sense himself:

"He has given us great promises by which we are made sharers of the divine nature." His gifts are all "grace," no matter what other wonderful names may describe them (peace, love, forgiveness, health, daily bread, etc.). And they are not given by the well-meant but rather pathetic transfer of title by which we try to make gifts to one another. For they are not from without, not external, not just things handed to us. They are divinely given; they are given creatively; they are part of the unbroken chain of creative love and power which is always the ground of our being.

When God gives us his peace, for instance, it is not merely that some external change is effected in our circumstances, though this may be also true. It is an internal gift to us: "not as the world gives"; it is given to our hearts. It is a divine enablement, a gift of creative power by which we are enabled to be peacemakers, both within our own soul and about us. We share the reality of God's peace, of peacefulness. His causing does not destroy our causing, but empowers it; his doing does not leave us passive, but active; we share his act, his freedom.

Thus the fruits of the Holy Spirit listed in St. Paul's familiar passage, charity, joy, peace, patience, etc., are all in a wonderful sense fruits of *our* soul, of *our* heart, too. They are not external decorations awarded to us; they are not external circumstances adjusted for us; they are not, in the final deep sense, *things* which we have received; they are life, grace, a true sharing in the divine nature. There is wonderful truth and dignity about God's gifts to us. They are *truly* given, not a mere "title," not a mere imputing, but a living creative sharing in the goodness of God.

Further, charity, joy, peace, patience, benignity, goodness, all these are not only *gifts* of Christ's Spirit; in a deeper sense, they *are* his Spirit. God does not just have love; God *is* love, God *is* joy, God *is* peace. Therefore, when we accept and live by his grace of charity, of joy, of peace, of patience, we accept God, we live by the Spirit of God, and God lives in us. "If anyone love me, he will keep my word, and my father will love him and we shall come and make our abode in him." And "I live now, not I, but Christ lives in me."

The more we live by the word of Christ, the more his Spirit will dwell in us. That is why we pray, "Come Holy Spirit, fill the hearts of your faithful." By receiving him we are enabled to receive him more and more, by possessing him we are able to desire him more and more. He teaches us to pray truly "in the name of Jesus." Indeed, the Spirit of Christ himself prays in us, "Abba, Father." He is the Paraclete, the Comforter; he is the Spirit of new creation, of life, of divine love and peace and truth. This is the wonder of our vocation, that it is *true,* that we are created for goodness, for truth and for love—that we are to be called, and to be, sons of God.

This fulfillment, this sanctification, is the special work of the Holy Spirit in us. Through him, by baptism and confirmation, we have been consecrated and sealed; through him the work of grace is begun in us; and according to St. Paul, "He whose power is at work in us is powerful enough, and more than powerful enough, to carry out his purpose beyond all our hopes and dreams." So that, in the end, all things are ours; and we are Christ's; and Christ is God's.

33 | Ourselves a Gift

In Chapters 14 to 17 of his Gospel, John records the beautiful and moving discourse of our Lord to his apostles at the Last Supper. Several times during that discourse our Lord repeats his promise to send his Holy Spirit to teach, to befriend, and to dwell continually with the disciples. Our Lord speaks of the Spirit he will send as the Spirit of truth. There is deep significance in this title, for it means both great joy to us and also the pain of our dying to falsehood. The joy comes because the work of the Holy Spirit in us is the work of true holiness, true sanctification. It is not a pretense of any kind, not even a divine pretense. The works of God are always true, and his work of sanctification in us is true also; our holiness becomes true holiness by our union with his Holy Spirit. Yet our way to holiness must also be by the painful way of the cross, because it means the hard task of detaching ourselves from all false goods. The heritage that comes to us in our fallen nature is a heritage of falsehood, from the father of lies. We are deceivers, and most of all we deceive ourselves. The development of our Christian vocation must always be, therefore, the development of our response to truth and the breaking away from falsehood.

But truth must spring from within, from the very depths of a man's heart, from that unique personal spirit in which he is created in the image and likeness of the true personal God.

This holy work of truth in man is in a special way the mission of the Holy Spirit whom Christ sends to us. Christ himself when he became incarnate in our humanity accepted our human nature in very truth, with all its natural limitations. He emptied himself that he might enter into the lowliness of creaturely existence, in time and in place and in all the finiteness which our weak nature knows. The holiness and the power of the eternal Word were indeed with him, but he fulfilled his mission of atonement and redemption through the weakness and suffering of a true man. In the sense in which he restored all creation to his Father by the infinite merit of his own personal oblation, he acted once and for all. But in the sense that his redemptive grace was to work unceasingly in every individual man and woman born into this world until the end of time, his sanctifying mission was to continue; and this was to be fulfilled in the Holy Spirit he would send. The Holy Spirit would not work through the physical humanity which Christ himself had accepted. The Holy Spirit would work with the freedom of the spirit, "breathing where he wills," acting upon men, not from without but from within, in the very fiber of their being. This is the supreme and unique power of the Creator's action upon his creatures, in that he alone operates in their whole being, not destroying the freedom and reason which he has bestowed, but indeed making these possible and actual by his creative power.

Every step in our Christian vocation, from our baptismal vows onward, is therefore a step toward truth. When we turn to Christ and ask to follow him, we are entering into the presence of perfect truth and perfect holiness, and asking to be made like him. We shall never fully understand either the wonder or the responsibility of our vocation until we contemplate the holiness of God in heaven and the completion of the transformation of grace in us: "Be perfect as your heavenly Father is perfect." Life can never be the same for those who have once set out to follow Christ, the Way, the Truth, and the Life. It is true that in coming to Christ we come to one of infinite compassion, mercy, and patience, infinite understanding and love. Yet, unlike the best of human friends, our Savior can never condone our falsehood and never let us finally rest in our untruth. Always he will be gently urging us, calling us, surrounding us, making his holy war upon us. He promises us indeed his peace, but not peace as the world gives peace, not false peace; and we shall only reach true peace when we learn to surrender wholly to his truth.

Our Lord *did* send his Spirit, as he promised, twenty centuries ago; and in all these years the teaching of Christ has developed in many remarkable ways. The mustard seed has grown into the great tree of his Church—an impressive tree, branching out into massive branches of dogma, moral theology, canon law, a most complex organization and administration, a sublime ritual of liturgical worship, and many concrete rules of spiritual life. This great tree grown from the seed of Christ's teaching has, in a sense, all the answers. Yet there is one answer that no system can provide, and in a way it is the only answer that finally matters: the personal answer of each soul to the word of God, the reality of the truth and the love in the heart. "God is a spirit, and those who worship him must worship him in spirit and in truth."

God's gifts reflect the truth and goodness of God himself. They seek no favors from us, no "deals"; they are the true symbols of his love for us, and invite only true love in return. They are given to us with a divine trust, handed over into our keeping and our use, for better or for worse. Thus, even before we consider the supernatural gifts of God, we find that we have great powers, great possibilities, great choices in our hands. The natural gifts of life and all life's powers are entrusted to us for our full acceptance and proper use. We have a right and a duty to develop according to our abilities and circumstances, manifesting our full character as human beings created in the image and likeness of God.

But the far greater supernatural gifts of God elevate us into a whole new way of being, a sharing in the life and activity of God himself. Yet these gifts also are entrusted truly and freely into our hands by God. We can freely choose and accept this new way of life, growing in friendship and knowledge of God, or we can waste and neglect and finally reject it. And the loss here is far more tragic than any loss of natural life or powers.

This is our true vocation then, to learn to know and rightly use the gifts of God, both the natural and supernatural gifts. And in the living individual person these are not two divided parts of life, but are to be drawn together, integrated, to form the whole person, the holy person. Therefore, in one of the great eucharistic prayers we beg: "O Lord, of your goodness make these gifts holy . . . and make us ourselves an eternal gift to your glory."

Corpus Christi

34 | He Puts His Whole Self into It

Every Mass is offered by the Church in joyful celebration of
our faith that the paschal gift of newness of life remains with
us till the end of time through the risen body of Christ in the
sacrament of the Eucharist. "Your fathers, who ate manna in
the desert, died none the less . . . I am the living bread . . . if
anyone eats of this bread he shall live forever . . . this bread is
my flesh, given for the life of the world." Every time we
gather to celebrate the Eucharist, we know that we are fulfilling the Lord's command. Our Lord himself said, "Do this in
remembrance of me," and gave us a great act to be done, a
great sign to be made effective, a sacrament to have true
meaning in our life.

The Blessed Eucharist is not offered to us as though it were
some specially holy relic of the Lord's body to be venerated.
Relics are remembrances and testaments of the dead, but the
Eucharist is a sign and act of the living Christ. It is the presence and the action of the living Christ in his people, and it is
the assembling and the acting of God's people in Christ. It is
a sign, above all others, of the life and union of Christ in and
with his people on this earth. Christian instinct has rightly
given the name "holy communion" to this sacrament, but has
not always rightly and fully understood the nature of this
communion. In our anxiety to defend the reality of Christ's
presence, "body and blood, soul and divinity," we have at

times moved toward a somewhat materialistic or mechanical concept of the Eucharist. We have perhaps seen it as a sacred *thing,* precious and holy, which when received would "do us good," and so the more often received the better. Yet, in fact, our own experience teaches us only too clearly that the mere multiplication of communions brings about little growth in true holiness. Indeed, the very phrase we use, to "receive" communion, is strange and revealing. Communion means an act between persons, not a thing that can be merely received. We do not speak of receiving conversation, receiving meeting, with our friends. Communion is an act of personal mutual relationship. It is alive, positive, a meaningful sign. It must mean something in us, not just a thing offered. "Real presence" itself implies this too, because we mean the presence of a person, not of a thing. And to be real and true, the presence of a person must be acknowledged, accepted, and reciprocated. Otherwise, that person is not really present to us, and his presence has no effect upon us.

Hence the real point and purpose of the Eucharist is not so much communion *of* Christ's body, but communion *with* his Spirit. It is not, in the deepest sense, a kind of mechanical nourishment of our soul through the mere assimilation of the body of Christ. It is to be a sign and means of grace effecting our true and living assimilation of and to his Spirit. It is to be an act of faith, of hope, of worship in spirit and in truth, and, above all, of supernatural charity: that is, of all that the true love of God and of the children of God must mean in our life. "Only the spirit gives life; the flesh is of no avail."

So the Blessed Eucharist was not really instituted just to consecrate the bread and wine into the body and blood of Christ. The sacraments are not given as ends in themselves; they are given for us, and they have their end in us. We should rather say, perhaps, that they serve the eternal ends of God by what they help to achieve in us here and now. While the bread and wine we bring to the altar are indeed consecrated into the body and blood of Christ, this is only in order to signify and achieve a far more wonderful, far more lasting consecration. It is not finally just the bread and wine that are to be consecrated; it is we ourselves, the living children of God, who are to be transformed and sanctified in this act of worship and love, who are to be by its help more and more truly consecrated to God's will.

This is not to be understood in a false and incomplete sense, as though we were saying there were only a "spiritual" presence of Christ here, as though the sacrament only *represented* ("signified" in the weak sense) Christ's presence. Communion is our sharing in the resurrected Christ; and the risen Christ was not just a spirit, but a most glorious and glorified man in all truth. He took food with his disciples, made them touch his victorious wounds. By God's creative and re-creative power, Christ rises from the dead the "firstborn" of all creatures, for the salvation of humanity, not of something substituted for it. Resurrection involves the totality of our being, spirit and flesh. And our union with Christ in the Eucharist is the supreme sign and instrument in this world of this totality of salvation. In the Eucharist we communicate with the living, risen Christ, body and blood, soul and divinity. And, as our Lord himself insisted: "Unless you eat of my flesh and drink my blood you shall not have life."

Even among ourselves, when we speak of gifts given to one another, especially when the gift is not a thing, but a loving service, something done for us, we often speak of a friend having "put so much love into it," and even of having "put himself into it." A mother figuratively "puts herself into" a special meal she prepares with love for her family. With Christ's creative love this becomes not just figuratively but ontologically true: he does put himself into his gift. So true and divine and self-giving is his loving service for us that there is indeed a true presence, the presence of a living, loving, acting Christ. Therefore, on our side, so must our eucharistic communion be a putting of ourselves into it: a true giving, a true presence, personal, aware, sincere, alive, and fruitful.

That is really the source of our eucharistic joy. In faith and hope we gratefully accept this great sacramental sign, and in humble love we try to realize and express its true meaning in our Christian life. Every communion is meant to be a wonderful fulfillment of our faith and baptism into Christ. Every communion is meant to be, not simply a mechanical receiving of his body, but a truly personal and meaningful putting on of Christ, that is, a communion with his Spirit. "Let this mind be in you which is in Christ Jesus." Christ gave himself in loving oblation to his Father's will for the redemption of all mankind. We are also called to give ourselves, following him in loving obedience to the Father's will and in loving service to all God's children, our brothers in Christ. With them too, our Eucharist must be a true and effective communion, a means to our "real presence" to each other.

35 | A Divine Compliment

Not long ago I was asked a question which on the surface may seem very simple, but actually touches a very profound mystery. It was this: "Why is it that when we are united to God in holy communion, all our sins and weaknesses are not utterly and overwhelmingly swept away by his infinite power and holiness?" This is a tremendous mystery, the encounter of our weak humanity with the infinity of God's power and holiness. Indeed, in a more frightening way, we might also ask why we ourselves in our sinful waywardness are not swept into nothingness by this confrontation with the Godhead. But, in different ways, both these questions point to mysteries of love; for all the mysteries of God are mysteries of infinite love. God has called us by personal vocation out of nothingness to share his life, his holiness, his love. We are his creatures, but he has made us creative creatures. We are not things, but persons made in the image and likeness of the personal God, reflecting the richness of personal life in unity which we call Trinity, three divine persons united in plenitude of life and love, a plenitude that flows out to us: "He has given us great promises by which we are made sharers of the divine nature."

It is precisely because of the dignity, truth, and beauty of this divine gift to us that it is neither mechanical nor overpowering. God destroys nothing that he has made, least of all the dignity of his creature and child, man: man in his human reality, a free reasonable person, choosing, willing, and above all, loving. Do not most of our troubles, even among ourselves, arise because we try to treat each other as things, not as persons? We try to impose our wills unreasonably; we *use* others selfishly, thus degrading them and destroying them. This can even come from a kind of distorted love, as in the overpossessiveness of parents toward their children, when they treat them as things, merely part of themselves, as in a false sense *their* children, and thus in fact tend to destroy them or, at least, as we say, to "spoil" them.

But God does not destroy or spoil the truth and dignity of the person that he has created and has wonderfully elevated by grace. In the miracles of Christ in his earthly life he exercised his power in two ways. One was with immediate and irresistible visible effect; this was over things: over blindness and disease, over winds and waves, over loaves and fishes, over death itself. The second was with mysterious restraint and respect; this was when he dealt with persons. He allowed his divine power to wait upon the dispositions of the heart. "If you can believe . . . Only believe and it shall be done . . . Much is forgiven her because she has loved much." He even allowed his divine power and love to be rejected. "The young man turned away and left him, for he had many possessions; and Jesus looked after him sorrowfully, for he loved him." He allowed himself to be rejected even by one of his chosen twelve; but, as he once asked the disciples, so he still asks us, "Will you also leave me?"

We do not understand the wonder and in a sense the vital necessity of the compliment that God pays us in treating us so. That poor word "compliment"; it has become so empty, often so insincere, and it is so inadequate here. For here it means something sublime and true: "I do not now call you servants but friends." Friendship, love, even divine love, cannot be forced, for then it is no longer love. It can only be freely given and freely returned. The precious gift of the nature in which God has created us is precisely that, by the truth of our free will and the dignity of our personality, he has enabled us to respond to him in friendship and love. We are not his things, but his children: "The Father desires those who worship him in spirit and truth."

The living sign of all this is Jesus Christ our Lord. He is the supreme sign, the supreme sacrament, the sacrament of the Incarnation; for he is true God and true man. In his person God and man meet. In the reality of his birth and life in our humanity, in the poignant events of his passion, death, and resurrection, the grace of our redemption is won. He came to live, to suffer, and to die for us, but not instead of us. Just as his divine mission was fulfilled in the truth and reality of his personal living and suffering for us on earth, so our divine vocation is to be worked out in our true personal living and laboring and loving. But now we are not alone; he abides in us by his grace and love. This is a spiritual, interior thing; but as a visible sign of this, as a sweet means of its increase, he has given us the Holy Eucharist. In this sacrament of his living body and blood we proclaim our adherence to him, to his word, to his law; and by this sacramental sign we truly communicate in his grace and holiness.

But it is as persons that we do this, not as mere receptacles. We share in his holiness and love according to our true personal desire and choice. But we know only too well how weak our desire proves to be, how strong our attachments to things other than him, the things of this world, of sense, of pride. So our communions are really a pledge of our renewed beginning again, of our renewed choosing of Christ, of our renewed conversion of life. As the sacramental sign of Christ's own passion, death, and resurrection, the Holy Eucharist helps us to communicate more and more truly with the Spirit of Christ, so that his divine power may indeed take possession of us and make us wholly his own.

36 | A God So Near

The joyful gift of the Blessed Eucharist is intended to bring the fruits of the passion, death, and resurrection of the incarnate Son of God to our individual souls, or, to put it the other way round, to bring us to God. Rightly used, the Blessed Eucharist is the principal means, on earth, of union with God. Rightly used, let us repeat, because not even the divine gift of the Eucharist produces its results automatically. The sacrament of the altar is not dependent on us for its own reality; but we must be aware of it and rightly disposed for it, if it is to have its sacramental reality and effect in our own soul, if it is to bring the incarnate love of God into oneness with us in personal reality.

With regard to our awareness of Christ's presence, we make the point rather insistently sometimes that the reality of his presence eludes our senses, that it is only by faith we come to him. But we ought not to fail to appreciate how wonderfully the sacramental signs of the Eucharist *do* meet our senses and, as it were, "focus" the divine presence of Christ for us. For, in a way far stronger and more vivid than any purely disembodied faith could bring to us, Christ comes to us, living and personal, through the signs of the Sacred Eucharist. "Blessed is he who comes," we sing at the Consecration; we know the moment of his coming; we know that he is with us. We meet him at the communion table; his priests carry him to us when we are sick; we come to the church to enter into his presence; we kneel before him in adoration and peace.

Yet, with all this, the Blessed Eucharist does remain a sign, a sign of faith. The outward signs of the sacraments do not mechanically compel in our minds proportionate and worthy dispositions. Rather, it is our faith which must guide our senses and interpret the signs. While the concrete signs, the "matter and form," of the sacraments do indeed wonderfully enkindle our affections, and so beautifully provide the needed "launching pad" for our faith, yet the sacramental mystery is far more effective, and remains far more undimmed by habit, than any merely natural sensible image could be. "This is the reason why the Holy Eucharist never grows common or usual; never ceases to stimulate our very senses. There is sufficient about it that it is palpable to give human faculty a foothold; but the grasp is the grasp of faith."*

What we fail to realize, even more than the divine presence in the Holy Eucharist, is the divine activity in it. It is Christ living, acting, continuing the loving work of the Incarnation, redeeming us, giving life, holiness, grace. It is part of the same unbroken chain of divine love that is eternally and infinitely active: the life of the Blessed Trinity, the creative outpouring that called us into being, the redemptive mission of the Incarnation, the daily bringing of that redemptive love to our souls by the sacrament of our altars. It is not merely God present to us, but God giving himself, and drawing us to himself, disposing us to turn to him, to cling to him,

* John Cuthbert Hedley, O.S.B., *A Retreat*, 16th ed. (Burns, Oates, and Washbourne, London; Newman Press, Westminster, Md.; 1951), p. 170.

to unite ourself to him. How rightly, therefore, is this sacrament called "holy *communion*."

In the touching, humble, yet so significant form of food, God unites himself to us through Christ and, by his grace, works upon our will so that we are united with him, by loving what he loves, doing what he commands. This is that newness of life, by which Christ lives in us and we in him, in charity, purity, oblation. "You have taken away our heart of stone and given us a heart of flesh."

After Pentecost

37 | Signs of His Presence

How faithfully the sacramental signs of the Church convey the presence and actions of Christ. In his corporal life on earth Christ had used signs too, those miracles which began the manifestation of his kingdom and called men to belief. After recording the miracle at Cana in Galilee, St. John writes: "This was the first of the signs given by Jesus; and he made known the glory that was his, so that his disciples learned to believe in him." But after our Lord had risen from the dead, in the full and free possession of divine power, he worked no more miracles in the physical order, but instituted the sacraments. These are now the signs by which we learn to know Christ, to come into his presence, to share his life of the Spirit.

Our Christian faith does not mean simply that we give our assent to the fact that certain events happened in the past, in the life of Jesus on earth; it is something far more vital. Faith is our belief that Christ is present and active in us now. When we make our profession of faith in the Apostles' Creed, we do indeed proclaim our belief in the historic reality of the specific facts of the incarnation, passion, and death of Jesus of Nazareth. But how often do we hurry through the second half of the Creed unthinkingly, as though it were the less important part. Yet, in one very practical way, it is the part that concerns us most. This is not to lessen the significance of the first part, but on the contrary to recognize the divine purpose of all those sublime events and to respond to them with a living faith. For it was not for his own sake that the Son of God was born of Mary, suffered under Pontius Pilate, was crucified, died, and rose from the dead. It was precisely that he might give to us, and that we might find faith and life in, "the Holy Spirit, the holy Catholic Church, the communion of saints, the forgiveness of sins, the resurrection of the body and life everlasting." Instead of rattling hastily through those final statements of our creed, we ought to proclaim them in a great solemn crescendo of joy, thanksgiving, and triumphant faith.

Because it was for this that he came: for us and for our salvation. And to us he has said: "Remember, I am with you always, until the end of the world." When Christ breathed his Spirit into the apostles, it was that they might preach his gospel to the whole world, exercising the work of salvation through sacrifice and sacraments. In the Spirit all mankind is to be drawn into the paschal mysteries of Christ's victory over sin and death. "To accomplish so great a work, Christ is always present in His Church" (Constitution on the Sacred Liturgy, Par. 7). It is with great force and clarity that the Council proclaims the living presence of Christ. The same paragraph continues: "He is present in the sacrifice of the Mass, not only in the person of His minister . . . but especially under the Eucharistic species. By His power He is present in the sacraments, so that when a man baptizes it is really Christ Himself who baptizes. He is present in his word, since it is He Himself who speaks when the holy Scriptures are read in the church. He is present, finally, when the Church prays and sings, for He promised: 'Where two or three are gathered together for my sake, there am I in the midst of them' (Mt. 18:20).''

The sacraments are the signs and the special means by which the Christian enters into the saving actions of Christ's passion, death, and resurrection thus wonderfully made present to us—or, rather, by which we are wonderfully taken up and made present to Christ's acts in their divine timelessness. But the sacraments are not the whole substance. All of Christian life is now taken up into Christ; all our knowing and loving and suffering is now truly his knowing and loving and suffering; the *admirabile commercium* of the Incarnation still continues, in its intimate exchange of divine and human. So that while there is indeed, thank God, an objective reality about the Church, visible in sacramental rites, visible as an institution in which we assemble to find redemption, truth, and charity, yet we must not reduce the Church nor limit the Spirit to ritual alone, to any mechanical sacramentalism. The liturgy of the Word is always present to remind us that God is only rightly worshiped in spirit and in truth, in the sincere personal service of our heart and life. All ritual is finally but a sign of our personal participation in the life and oblation of Christ; but it is meant to be an effectual sign.

So the true sacramental character of the Church has a threefold dimension: there is the divine action of Christ himself in the ritual; there is the true ministerial service of the priesthood; and there is the loving personal commitment of all the members in faith. The action of Christ himself will never fail; he will always be with us; and his Church is therefore, in him, indefectible. But the priestly service and the personal commitment may indeed fail, both in fidelity and in relevance, and so the Church will also be ever in need of reform and renewal. Furthermore, the Church is not a closed corporation, but must always be open and calling to all men, working for that solidarity of all men already wonderfully begun in Christ. There must never be any sense of exclusiveness in the Christian assembly, for the sacrifice of the cross embraces all men, and the eucharistic remembrance of that sacrifice must mean communion with all men in Christ. That is the true sign of his presence.

38 | So Also I Send You

The opening words of the Decree on Priestly Formation issued by the Second Vatican Council state that "the wished-for renewal of the whole Church depends in large measure on a ministry of priests which is vitalized by the spirit of Christ." We know, of course, that in the ultimate and strictest sense God does not need, is not dependent on, a human priesthood. The essential bond between God and his children is an interior, invisible one. God can draw man to himself, can communicate his divine life, his Holy Spirit to the soul; and man, by God's enabling grace, can respond, can worship and love. Yet in fact God has always willed to use a visible ministry, a mediation, an outward dispensation. The Incarnation itself is the supreme witness that God willed to make himself personally and visibly known to men, "for through the mystery of the Word made flesh, a new light of your glory shone upon our mind, so that while we acknowledge him as God seen by men, we may be drawn by him to the love of things unseen" (Christmas Preface). But even this could have been limited to the sacred humanity of Christ himself in his life on earth, leaving an unforgettable memory, a profound teaching, a sublime example for all time to come. Yet the Son of God chose, in fact, that his personal ministry and presence should continue in a way which, in a different sense, we can almost call incarnate, because sacramental, in a way our nature needs, in his Church.

Christ's Church and Christ's priests are to continue his
ministry in those ways by which the Son of God on earth
drew men to the life of the invisible Godhead: through concrete personal things, not through mere theories and philosophical ideals. Christ brought eternal life into our world,
into our time and place, into human life as we know it. For
our nature is so weak, so darkened, that the great things of
the spirit, even of God's Spirit, easily escape us, are excluded
by the apparently closer, more urgent realities of sense. So
they have to be brought down to us, somehow embodied for
us and in us, in human experience. And thus Christ became
man "desiring to consecrate the world," to establish the kingdom of God, to turn all to grace. He came not to bring mystery but revelation, not to tell us of a distant God but to bring
God close. And how sweetly, wonderfully close was the Godhead to mankind in Christ!

But all men have need of this closeness, not only those
whose privilege it was to experience directly what St. John
described: "What our own eyes have seen, our hands
touched." Therefore, in the merciful providence of truly
divine wisdom and love, Christ said to men, "As the Father
has sent me, so also I send you." The work of the incarnate
Son of God was to continue on earth, not merely in historical
record and example, but by living human agents, renewed
and succeeding through generation after generation. There
was to be a visible Church, a living word, a daily ministration
of sacrifice and sacrament, an apostolic succession: "I will be
with you all days, until the end of the world." The first work
of the priest, then, is to bring eternal life and truth into his
own time and place; he is sent to those around him, into
definite, particular conditions of ordinary human life. And,
in so doing, he is to be their salvation!

Christ came to men as person to person—not as a book or letter or sign, but face to face, eye to eye, in the living presence of personal individual relationship. Men do not live or die for an abstraction, for a law, a theory. We live or die for a person. It was the person of Christ, the eternal Word of God in his humanity, that made men like Simon, Andrew, Levi, leave everything to follow him. It is him we love, him to whom we are drawn. We can hardly say why this is so. His teaching is difficult; his demands, it might seem at times, impossible. Yet "to whom else should we go?" Even with our human friends we experience a like situation. It is not really their words or their actions that draw us finally; it is they themselves, the persons that they are. In the person of the eternal Word of God, something of the divine beauty and goodness of Christ comes through, even to us. And somehow (and this is a humbling, frightening thing for a priest) the personal Son of God has to come to men now, and men have to be drawn to him now, through the person of the priest. Somehow the priest, by his living personal ministry, his presence, his powers, has to exert that living pressure and attraction on men which is to bring them, not to himself (that is always the dangerous diversion), but to his Master, the personal God to whom they belong, whom they need.

And this suggests another way by which the incarnate God called men to himself, namely by the way of humility, without which there can be no communion of man with God. The Son of God came on earth poor, lonely, suffering, a failure, so that no man who was not willing to renounce pride, ambition, avarice, could follow him: "That seeing they may not perceive, hearing they may not understand." Christ took this terrible risk in order that men's motives might be true. And so it is with the priesthood of the Church.

If men must seek God by coming to a man, by confessing their sins, by obeying visible authority, by humbling their minds to learn like little children from a mind less gifted than their own, then already they are strongly led into the spirit of Christ's gospel and away from the proud spirit of the world. Thus, the very existence of priests among men is a kind of witness to faith, and to Christ.

We have been thinking about the priesthood in its special sense of sacramental orders. But every one of us who is baptized into Christ shares his priesthood in a profound and beautiful way. We share his worship, his oblation, his sacrifice, his redemptive mission, his unceasing apostolate. In the words of St. Peter: "Set yourselves close to him, so that you too, the holy priesthood that offers the spiritual sacrifices which Jesus Christ has made acceptable to God, may be living stones, making a spiritual house . . . You are a chosen race, a royal priesthood, a consecrated nation, a people of God." This is our divine vocation; this is the source of all our hope and joy.

39 | The Vine and the Branches

An often-quoted remark of G. K. Chesterton is his comment: "Christianity has not failed; it has never been tried." That may exonerate the theory of Christianity, but it is a devastating condemnation of Christians. And, in any case, Christianity is not a theory; it is the active enterprise of a living body. It is an existing Church; it exists in us its members. So if we have never even tried, Christianity is indeed an utter failure. This has always been the stumbling block, from St. Peter's cowardly denial to our own daily failure in Christian witness and love. But it is more than ever crucial in our own generation. Men have lost patience with words; they demand deeds. There exists a strong social conscience which is acutely aware of the problems of peace and war, civil rights, international justice, ignorance, and poverty. And many people have turned away in impatience and disgust from the lethargy, the ineffectiveness, and even, they feel, the hypocrisy of the churches in the face of these tasks. Rightly or wrongly, they have taken scandal, hearing only words, and sometimes not even words when words should be spoken out clearly; and they see few effective deeds.

What can we say to all this? First, surely, we must humbly confess much personal failure and much failure as a Church, as a people of God sent to work for his kingdom in this world. We do recognize that most of us have never *really* tried

Christianity, that is, never tried to practice it with our whole heart and soul. For this is the challenge which many of our Lord's hard sayings refer to: "If any man would come after me, let him take up his cross and follow me. He who loves his own life shall lose it; he who hates his own life shall gain it." This is the sharing in Christ's total oblation, for love of the Father and of men: to give oneself away. The saints practiced this kind of folly, the folly of the cross, of wholehearted love. Christianity is fairly easy to live respectably, sensibly, comfortably; it is very hard to live totally, with the whole heart; it is very hard to give oneself away.

Yet we are all called to follow Christ; we are all invited to love with our whole strength, to give with our whole heart. This is the deepest meaning of our vocation as Christians: "You must be a holy priesthood, to offer up that spiritual sacrifice which God accepts through Jesus Christ." This Christian priesthood is not primarily some mysterious active participation in liturgical sacrifice; it is our sharing in Christ's personal sacrifice. Christ's real sacrifice was the sacrifice of his human personal life, in his poverty, his toil, his solicitude, his love, his suffering, his courageous defense of the innocent and oppressed. In all this there was perfect obedience to his Father's will, even when it was distorted by the injustice and cruelty of men, even to the death of the cross. This was Christ's own priestly sacrifice: the gift of himself in spirit and in truth, in obedience and love for God and men. And what was true for Christ is true for his followers. In him we, too, are enabled to offer true priestly worship, to offer our own personal sacrifice in the loving gift of ourselves. This deep essential priesthood is identified with the twofold love of God and of man, and is the reality underlying the ritual priesthood of liturgy. The sacraments are *signs* of the deeper reality, of the life of God in us, the life of faith and charity; they are not the life itself.

So the priestly people of Christ is not primarily a people set apart from the world, assembled in God's temple for ritual mysteries. Their priestly mission is to sanctify the world by that spiritual sacrifice in their own life which continues Christ's work of redemption and consecration and builds up his kingdom. Otherwise, there is danger that the liturgy may become a substitute for the reality of Christian life, rather than a sign and instrument of it. Our satisfaction in renewing the liturgy could become an escape from the work of renewing the world, from the sacrifices needed for the hungry and the poor and the oppressed. "For all their works, prayers, and apostolic endeavors, their ordinary married and family life, their daily labor, their mental and physical relaxation, if carried out in the Spirit, and even the hardships of life, if patiently borne—all of these become spiritual sacrifices acceptable to God through Jesus Christ (cf. 1 Pet. 2:5). During the celebration of the Eucharist, these sacrifices are most lovingly offered to the Father along with the Lord's body. Thus, as worshipers whose every deed is holy, the laity consecrate the world itself to God." (Dogmatic Constitution on the Church, Par. 34.)

Therefore, in order to continue Christ's redemptive mission in this world as his priestly people, we are incorporated in him by faith and baptism, nourished by his Eucharist, taught by his word, guided by his authority. That is, we are gathered together in his Church, a vulnerable institutional organization. We have somehow managed to separate the ideas of the priesthood of liturgy and the priesthood of mission and charity, whereas in reality they are bound together and interdependent. To proclaim the gospel is to offer worship, to offer love of God and love of man in such a way as to draw other men into this same true worship. This evangelization demands a clear commitment to the great tasks of the world in our day. Men will not accept witness which seems to evade the full responsibilities of a truly human life. The Eucharist itself is meant to strengthen us, to send us out on our mission each day among men, to enable us to share more fully in Christ's universal redemptive love and in his saving mission.

We read in the gospel that if at the altar we remember that our brother has some claim against us, we must leave our offering and go first to be reconciled, and this may sometimes be literally necessary. But the procedure also works the other way round. The sacramental Eucharist is meant to enlighten and strengthen our supernatural life and love, and thus to send us to be reconciled with, or to work for, our brothers. In Christ we find the courage and wisdom to face life; we find divine life and love itself. And it is only in him that we really have anything to give. If we forget this, we are in danger of reducing the gospel of salvation to a mere humanism, a frail ideal of our own sinful nature. Our Christian Church would then be just a humanitarian association. But the Church is the living body of Christ; and our hope lies wholly in the living person of Jesus Christ, true God and true man, who took our flesh for our redemption. Our salvation rests in our incorporation in him, always living in his Church; and in him we, too, are called to be a "living sacrifice, holy and acceptable to God."

This is the Christian paradox: our salvation is totally the gift of God's love in Christ; yet in Christ man is enabled to cooperate and receive God's gift actively and freely. Without

Christ we can do nothing; with him we can live and act divinely. We become partners in the whole divine enterprise, the salvation of the whole world. This is to bear fruit from the good tree in which we are implanted, Jesus Christ, the true vine.

40 | What Do You Seek?

Three times during their first year in a Benedictine monastery, the novices come before the abbot, in the presence of all the community, and in reply to the question "What do you seek?" they answer: "Perseverance, Father." The abbot then addresses to them some words of encouragement, but also warns them of the difficulties of the religious state. It might be useful to apply this little custom to every walk of Christian life, for, although there is special reason for young men to consider well the difficulties of the religious state before they bind themselves to it by vows, every state of life has its own difficulties.

One reason for trying to recognize and foresee difficulties is not that we should be deterred and try to escape them, but rather that we should be prepared for them, that we should know how to meet and use them. It is often the difficulties, at least as much as the easy successes, which are the material of our sanctification. For it is the difficulties that show up the deficiencies in our character, show us what we are, and offer us the opportunity of conversion of life. They offer us more clearly, usually, the choice between God's will and our own; they are a test of whether we are truly seeking God or ourselves. When all is going smoothly, we may complacently feel that we are serving God alone; but when the setbacks, the misunderstandings, the contradictions, the failures, come along, there may be exposed our personal vanities, our self-will, our impatience, and all kinds of other imperfect motives and characteristics which success might not have revealed.

Therefore, difficulties of all kinds are often the most fruitful occasions of our conversion of life. Admittedly, this conversion is our lifelong task and will never be ended, but the important thing is that it should be honestly begun. And this requires two basic dispositions in us: first, a willingness to learn; second, a generous attempt to put into effect what we learn. Neither of these is easy. Although there is a strong instinct in man to want to learn, yet he does not like to be taught his own faults. And by faults we mean not just those obvious lapses which must often be recognizable even to ourselves, but rather the predominant faults in our character; we mean not so much what we *do,* as what we *are.* To learn this, we need great humility, and great faith in God and in our fellow men.

But even when we do manage, in some part, to recognize our own faults of character, we still have another difficult task: namely, to form a sincere and effective will to change, to put into practice what we know is really promised by our conversion. This is not a matter of some superficial religious etiquette, but the changing of our real self, our personality, our inmost mind and heart. We know that by the fruitful blessings of his grace, as well as by the purifying and pruning effects of our tribulations, our heavenly Father is cultivating our soul, leading us to growth in holiness. What fruit is the seed of the divine word bearing in us?

Both the Church's liturgy and the monastic rule teach that sacrifice and joy go together. Sacrifice consists in that external worship we owe to God, particularly rendered to him through the liturgy, and in that internal oblation of our will to him, that true interior worship of sincere conversion of life. This last is beautifully depicted in Psalm 118: "I will meditate on your commandments, which I have loved exceedingly, and lift up my hands to your commandments, which I have loved." And this sacrificial seeking of God leads to true joy: "Let the heart of them that seek the Lord rejoice." The mark of those who seek God is not sadness, not dejection, but patience, cheerfulness, peace. If we are truly seeking God alone, we shall find peace and happiness; but insofar as we are in some way seeking ourselves, some compromise between God and our disordered self, then we shall find conflict, discouragement, sadness. The important question, then, is whether we surrender to our weakness and seek consolation in indulging ourself in some way, or whether we try to recognize what is happening, to renew and purify our seeking for God, to turn our will once more, bravely, toward him.

"Seek the Lord alone, seek the Lord always, seek his face in sincerity and truth." The one question that St. Benedict asks of those who would follow his Rule might well be asked by every Christian: Do I truly seek God? This is the way of Christ, the way of unselfish love, of humility and obedience, but also of peace and joy.

41 | The Truth Shall Make You Free

The essence of the Christian life will always be the true personal response of the heart of man to God. But our life fulfills itself in a strange tension between individual and community, freedom and law. Truth is not some arbitrary subjective concept of the individual man, but the right perception and acceptance of the objective realities about us. And, as the scriptures themselves assure us, it is truth that will make us free.

For the purposes of Christian spiritual life, it is useful to consider freedom from two points of view. The first might be called freedom from the law, in the sense used by St. Paul as he tried to make men understand that salvation is the gift of God's love bestowed through Christ, not the result of legal observances. At the Apostle's time this referred mainly to preoccupation with the requirements of the Mosaic law. We are no longer involved in the same disputes about dietary prescriptions, ritual cleansings, circumcision, and the rest; but the Apostle's teaching remains relevant for us too, because there is always a strong tendency in us to reduce religion to mere legal observance. We feel uncomfortable about the immeasurable and in some ways indefinable character of true religion, which our Lord described as worship in spirit and in truth, as loving God with our whole heart. These are simple and beautiful words, but their fulfillment on this earth is most difficult and complicated. We do not like this unqualified vocation, this "seventy times seven" challenge; and we are tempted to seek security by reducing religion to definite legal observances. The question "What must I do to be saved?" may not always be asked in the right way. It may really mean no more than "Am I safe if I observe certain practices?" But it is always dangerous for religion to become identified with observances and things, because it is first a grace of personal relationship between the living Spirit of God and the living spirit of man. It must sometimes be expressed in laws and observances and ceremonies, but it must not be identified with them.

That is why the Church herself, every now and again, has to have a renewal, a kind of "shake-up" out of our habits of settling for mere things instead of for spirit and truth. So, suddenly, fish on Friday is out; Lenten fasts are voluntary; Latin is no longer a sacrosanct language; and church organs find themselves in competition with guitars. Some of these changes come as a shock to our settled habits; and, in a way, they are meant to. Admittedly, too, they often involve genuine difficulties, especially when we seem to be left with neither one thing nor the other. For we are not disembodied spirits, and we do need these things or something like them. And after the shake-up we still have to return to the help of laws, of sacraments, of words and actions, in order to express our worship and our faith. It is no easy task to find the right things, the right words, the right ways. But this pain is a price we must pay to preserve our freedom from things, freedom from "the law," from a kind of idolatry; it is a price we pay to preserve our freedom to worship in spirit and in truth. "You are not under law but under grace."

But there is also a second, quite different aspect to Christian freedom, which we might call freedom from the world, from the slavery of sin and of selfishness. This also is a most urgent and true quality of the freedom of the children of God. It is the sort of freedom that our Lord must have meant, at least in part, when he spoke of the blessedness of the poor in spirit. For true poverty makes a man free, makes a man open to the word of God and to the riches of his kingdom. One of the great signs that Christ cited in answer to John the Baptist's question whether he was indeed the Messiah was that the poor had the gospel preached to them. It is not, surely, that the rich are to be excluded from the message of salvation, but that to hear the word of God all men first need humbly to recognize their true poverty and true need of God. They need the simplicity and humility of the poor of heart. The kingdom that the Messiah is proclaiming is not the power of this world; it is the kingdom of heaven, of the Father, and its essential message is the word of faith.

And yet we must go on at once to say that the kingdom of God is not, as it were, detached from this world; it is not cut off from the reality of our human life. It is truly incarnate amongst us, real and concrete and embodied in us: "The kingdom of God is among you." The miracle of the multiplication of the loaves and fishes was not only a great messianic sign of the bread of heaven and the kingdom to come; it was also effectual there and then. The poor were not sent away empty, with *only* the promise of heavenly reward; the hungry were really fed by the wayside.

And the Christian Church today, while in one sense its first task is to preach the kingdom of heaven, is also necessarily involved in this world. We cannot preach the justice of God

without also working for justice among men; we cannot teach
men to be content with their state in life if that is a state of
inhumanity unworthy of the image of God in which they
were created. Our Lord sternly rebuked the Pharisees for
laying unbearable legal burdens upon men without themselves lifting a finger to help them. The message of the
Church of Christ does indeed look beyond this world, but it
does not ignore this world. It teaches men to see the goodness
of temporal things, but to judge them according to standards
of eternal goodness.

The Church has always been and will always be concerned
with the condition of men in this world. This holds true at
all levels of the Church: the magisterial social encyclicals of
the popes, of Leo, Pius, John, and Paul; the active welfare
campaigns of the bishops; the dedication of the religious
orders; and, most of all, the loving Christian service of all the
faithful people of God to their fellow men. But because all of
these, popes, bishops, religious, and faithful, are themselves
also in and of this world, their achievement is always imperfect, their attitude sometimes heartless, blind, weak; so there
is much sad failure in the mission of Christ's Church on
earth. This is indeed grievous and can never be condoned,
but only sorrowfully confessed and amended. But we are not
left without consolation even here, if we return to the other
great aspect of the Church's message, namely, that she is after
all concerned finally with the kingdom of heaven: Blessed are
you poor, you who suffer; your reward will be great in
heaven. Again, this is not to excuse injustice and neglect and
inhumanity here and now, but it is to comfort the suffering
with the knowledge that all this passes away, that the only
abiding kingdom is the kingdom of the Father. And although
much of our work here, even in his Church, may fail, his

work will not fail. He will not send the poor away empty, but will fill the hungry with good things. Nothing escapes the final solution of his providence; nothing can finally silence the words with which the Son calls the sufferer home: "Come you blessed of my Father, yours is the kingdom of heaven."

42 | That My House May Be Filled

Part of the reason for all the present unsettledness of religion is that many people, especially young people, are intensely preoccupied with thoughts of personal responsibility, integrity, and sincere individual and social commitment. This is in itself very good and desirable. We are in strong reaction against over-conventionalized religious practices, over-mechanical sacramentalism, and depersonalized observance of law.

We are anxious now that our obedience should be an intelligent and reasonable service, involving worthy personal commitment to an urgent cause. We are anxious that our faith should be an enlightened personal assent to doctrine that is presented with openness and truth. We are anxious that our charity should build upon generous human friendship and respect for human rights. All these anxieties are surely proper, and arise from too much misunderstanding in the past. If we think of the word "charity," for example, which ought to be the warm living heart of Christian behavior, we cannot but recognize how men have succeeded in degrading and impoverishing the word until it is almost an insult. The word now suggests misfortune, humiliating handouts, whether for the body or for the spirit. To live by charity is to come to a pitiful state indeed. There is no doubt that there is a genuine, deep instinct motivating the present heart-searching and the reaching out toward true Christian ideals.

We have only one life, not two; we are only one person, not two; we have only one deep life source for all our actions, the immortal spirit within us. Our religious activity is not really separate from our human activity; our supernatural life is not really separate from our natural life. The divine grace is to be very exactly embodied in our actual being. There is only one great commandment: to love God with all our heart and all our strength and all our soul—and our neighbor as ourself. Therefore, I fervently thank God for all the present earnest striving to make our liturgical service true personal worship, both by the individual and by the whole group; to make our sharing in the eucharistic sacrifice and charity of Christ go forth from the altar to all Christ's brothers everywhere, in loving recognition of them and their needs; to make our religious faith a vital personal and intelligent commitment to truth, with convictions at least as strong as those with which we direct our businesses and our pleasures.

But having said this, I do want to mention another idea along somewhat different lines. All of the preceding is, as it were, for our stimulation and personal awakening; what follows is more for our humble thanksgiving and consolation—though not, I hope, a mere tranquilizer. It is this. Around and within all that vital personal consciousness in religion there flows continually the strong tide of the mighty power of Christ's own redemptive mercy. Without in any way denying the reality and truth of our freedom of personal response to grace, we joyfully and thankfully feel the creative force of divine love carrying us along. Indeed, how could we underestimate the victory of the incarnate Son of God? His bright sacrifice gathers up all our sacrifices and all our hesitations into the fire of his love. We must indeed be concerned and sincere about the truth of our decisions and choices. But, in a way, it seems that divine love has made many of these decisions for us. It was his creative will, not our own, that brought us out of nothingness into life, that brought us out of darkness into faith, that brought us out of sin into grace. Many of our decisions, even in daily life, are at least shaped for us by his providence. And think of that last great decision of all, the decision of death, the step we all must take in order to pass into the fullness of life. How many of us would have the strength for this decision if his love did not mysteriously compel us? "Go out into the highways and hedgerows, and give them no choice but to come in, that my house may be filled."

So it seems to me that there is this rather wonderful twofold character in our life. On the one hand, there is the wonderful challenging invitation of God's grace to make a wholly personal, true, free response from an enlightened mind and a loving will. On the other hand, since he also knows our weaknesses, there is his own constant abiding presence and action within us and about us, as he promised, guiding us, protecting us, leading us, even compelling us along the road of his love. And thus each of us learns, humbly and gratefully, that it is not easy to escape from his strong hands.

I will add just this final thought. We are at present emphasizing the reality of the Blessed Eucharist as the great sacrificial and sacramental action of Christ, and we are rather de-emphasizing what might be thought of as the more passive presence of Christ as the "prisoner of love in the tabernacle." Well, there is reason for this, as that very phrase at once shows. But, still, let us remember that the abiding presence of our Redeemer in the blessed sacrament of the altar is a sign of that never ceasing current of divine love, mercy, and providential care which is always within and about us, saving us almost in spite of ourselves, in spite of all the poor weaknesses and failures in our own personal response. "Peace be with you! It is I, do not be afraid."

43 | Light in Darkness

Suffering is never very far from us in this life, either in ourselves or in those close to us; and every now and then we are brought face to face with it in some more piercing way. Our only ultimate and invincible resource when we meet the mystery of suffering close at hand is our desperate humble prayerful trust in the God of love, the God of goodness and wisdom. That we must always come back to; that must be always there. But sometimes, when troubles are not so pressing, we may be able to philosophize a bit about it, and even get some little glimpse of what is (dare we say it?) "gained." Especially does this apply to the anguish of perseverance in prayer, when no answer, no relief seems to be given.

Think for a moment of the famous example of the prayers and tears and heartache of St. Monica. For fifteen or twenty years, from her son's adolescence on, this woman of faith and love prayed and prayed for the conversion of Augustine. He had never been baptized; he was leading an irregular life; he was following ways of intellectual error. She prayed for his conversion, that he might accept baptism, that he might become a good husband and father. The years went on; her prayers went on; and her prayer seemed unheard. Then, when Augustine was thirty-three, came his conversion and baptism, and all that followed. If Monica's prayer had been answered easily and quickly, perhaps Augustine would have been just what she was asking for: a good son, a faithful husband and father. And perhaps she herself would have become a fond, complacent, even possessive, mother. But her prayer was only answered after long perseverance, much anguish of heart, much hoping against hope. But then, finally, how wonderfully! What fruit that humble persevering prayer finally bore in God's grace! Augustine became not just a good son to her, but a good and great son to her Church; not just a faithful father of a family, but a great bishop, Doctor, and Father of the Church; not just a respectable parishioner, but a saint of God. And Monica, too, joined the ranks of the saints. Yes, sometimes we do catch a ray of divine light and wisdom through a dark cloud of suffering that finds a reflection even in our poor worldly minds; and we are helped to renew and deepen our patient hope and faith.

I suppose that a basic point in our thinking about the problem of evil is that we must acknowledge that God's creation is real, is true. God is not some stage God, lurking in the wings of an unreal melodramatic world, always rushing in to rescue everybody, turning everything into a kind of farcical pretense in which the actors are only puppets. No, creation has more truth and dignity to it than that; and God destroys nothing that he has made, including the reality and the consequences of our acts and choices, even though the price of this is sometimes pain. Our Christian trust in God's providence does not teach us to pretend heartlessly that pain and trouble of all kinds are not a real and heavy burden on our humanity. But it does teach us to believe that nothing finally escapes the embrace of God's goodness and love, that through it all, through the pain as well as through the joy, the final outcome is ruled by God. And his purposes are all purposes of happiness and love. So we start with a kind of twofold acceptance. First, we accept the reality and in some sense the inevitability of suffering, now that sin has brought tragic disorder into our world; and secondly, we accept far more firmly the hope that the infinite wisdom of God is turning all to the eternal ends of love. Ours it is to struggle with the transitory means; it is God's prerogative to govern the end.

But then we can go on to a second step in our philosophizing. When we are trying to cope somehow with children (of all ages), we are often very well satisfied (as well as exhausted) when we get them to accept the *principle* of some rule, of unselfishness, of coming home at reasonable hours, of obedience, and so on. Once we have gained their acceptance of the principle, we sometimes feel able to allow exceptions in special cases—"just for this once." So too may we turn to our heavenly Father with all our fervent prayers for our special needs and "exceptions." We acknowledge the principle that we must bear our part in the sad chronicle of the evils that afflict our humanity now: sickness, poverty, fear, death itself. Yet, while humbly recognizing the principle and the justice of our suffering for sin, whether our own or others, we do most earnestly turn to God in our distress to beg for relief and help, especially for his care of those most dear and close to us. We know that sorrow is really the lot that man chose for himself when he turned away from God by sin; but we cannot help saying, "But Lord God, it *is* still your world; you cannot disclaim responsibility for it; these are your dearly loved children, your friends whom you love; save them, save them!" Principles are true and good, but we are right not to take no for an answer in particular cases; we must continue to ask with all our heart, even though somewhere deep down in that heart we are also trying to say, "Thy will be done." And, perhaps more often than we remember, these prayers are answered; our dear ones are spared; our troubles somehow pass.

But then, finally, what do we do when all our philosophizing breaks down, when only the darkest side of trouble is upon us, when no prayer seems heard, when anguish seems heaped on anguish? *Then* is the time of faith; then is the time of hope—hoping against hope. Help thou my unbelief; help thou my hopelessness! No longer do we understand; no longer do we see how even tomorrow will be livable, or see any tomorrow. Yet, somehow we must cut through it all, not to the God of philosophy, not to any reasoning, but to the living God of faith, to the living Son of God who became incarnate to share and transform our sufferings, to make them—by a truly divine transformation—the special instrumentality of redemption and holiness and love. When things are really bad, there is only one way for us to turn: to the living, loving Christ who somehow invites us to trust him and to share with him the mystery of the cross, so that we may share with him the greater mystery and unimaginable joy of his resurrection.

44 | With Minds Made Clean

Prayer is an inexhaustible subject, and we can never say everything about it, nor indeed anything really worthy of this mysterious grace and privilege of the children of God. Although it is in essence "ineffable," "beyond words," it is always possible to offer *some* words—both about prayer and in our own personal prayer.

It is true that there sometimes seems to be a lack of true relationship between the formal words we are saying and the personal sentiments of our heart. And perhaps we think that it is the words which are, as it were, false, and that we should abandon them for the truer feelings of our heart; but this is not always right. Sometimes it is the words which are really true, and our hearts which are not able to perceive and make this truth their own. The point of persevering in formal prayer, therefore, is that our hearts may be changed, rather than the words.

This would probably be a rather difficult and dry procedure, however, if this were all there were to our prayer; and we should soon be discouraged. So as well as this perseverance in more formal prayer, we need some element of more spontaneous and interior prayer, and this immediately suggests the time-tested practice of bringing spiritual reading into prayer. The ancient tradition about this kind of prayer can be summed up in three words: reading, meditation, prayer.

This reading must be primarily "spiritual," that is, not *merely* for intellectual or theological enlightenment. It is our seeking of the spirit of God through the word of God, not that we may know *about* him but that we may *know him* in order to worship him. Therefore, its manner will be slow and repetitive, as well, of course, as humble and sincere. This is not the very systematic meditation of the more modern "methods of prayer," but a more spontaneous reflection and reaction of our spirit to the word of God. And this leads into the third element, interior prayer, when for a moment our soul perceives the light of divine truth and assents to it, when our heart senses the divine goodness and responds to it in love. It is, as far as is possible in this life, a moment of personal contact with God; it is part of our personal response to our personal vocation as children of God. On God's side, it is his gift, his communication of himself to us. That is what makes it possible; that is what sometimes even makes it easy. On our side, perhaps the clearest element is "consent," acceptance, the willingness to "listen to God." It really goes beyond words or argument; it is immediate, spontaneous, certain. It is the response of our deepest self to God, the ground of our being; it is our joyful echo of divine truth and goodness. These moments of prayer may be brief, but they are also true. From them we return to our reading and our meditation and await the renewal of divine light and warmth.

As to "difficulties in prayer," do not let *that* discourage us! The wonder is, not that we find it difficult to pray, but that we manage to pray at all! Prayer is *not* natural to us; it is *super*natural, and in a way we are quite out of our element in it. It is not just a matter of acquiring a new skill, a new technique. We are always tempted to think that if only we could discover the right "method," all our difficulties would be over. But prayer is not just a psychological attainment; it is part of our whole new way of existing by the life of Christ in us. It is part of our lifelong vocation to put off the old man and to put on the new man, to "make way" for the Spirit of Christ in us. God knows our frailty and our complexity and our darkness. He does not look for perfect prayer from us, but he does call us to seek him humbly and perseveringly through the attempt of prayer. It is really our desire and our attempt that matter, not our "success."

There is doubtless very much more to prayer than the very simple steps suggested here. Yet I think this can be a beginning of prayer; and in prayer the great thing really is *to begin.* The Holy Spirit can lead us on. And if we persevere faithfully, then these moments of grace will be multiplied and will lead us to that state of prayerfulness in which our mind and heart will always tend toward God. Then our daily work and occupations will be seen in the light of God's truth and the warmth of God's goodness; for somehow, St. Paul tells us, "we are not to be like those whose minds are set on the things of earth, for our conversation is in heaven."

45 | The Redemption of Work

A very large slice of our life, of our time, our strength, our health, our interest, goes into our work. And since our life is given to us for one purpose only—to know, love, and serve God—it is obvious that somehow or other our work should play a large part in this knowing and loving and serving God. Otherwise, one big part of our life is fulfilling no purpose. Yet a good many people come to the practical conclusion that work is nothing more than a necessary evil in their life, a negative thing at best, an unredeemable condition of this world, of which the least said the better. They feel that the only possibility of spiritual life and growth lies in a part of their life utterly detached from their workaday existence.

When we remember the kind of occupation that so many people have to earn their living by, the impersonal and de-humanized routine of factory or office, so uncreative, so unful-filling, moving only by the artificial limbs of business, it is not hard to understand why many give up any attempt to see a connection between their work and the eternal purpose for which they were created. But is there some part of human life which is unredeemed and unsanctified by Christ's redemptive sacrifice? Would our Lord really have left such a large part of man's life outside the realm of his grace? What is the answer?

I believe that the difficulty about sanctifying our work arises out of two quite contrary conditions. One arises along the lines I have already mentioned, when the occupation is so inhuman, so unworthy of our higher faculties, that it seems impossible to raise it to the supernatural level. The other arises when, on the contrary, the occupation is so human, when it fulfills our natural gifts and powers so satisfactorily, that we altogether forget to raise it to the supernatural level. Instead of working for the glory of God, we are, more or less unwittingly, working for our own satisfaction, that is, for our own self-will or some other appetite. How can we avoid this seeming dilemma?

Well, for one thing, there is our motive: the motive of divine charity. Somehow or other, deep down, our work must be done for love of God. This does not mean emotional fervor, but an attempt to find in our work the divine will. Service of God without love would only be slavery, unwilling drudgery; this is not at all what he invites us to in the vocation of children of God. How many times St. Paul reminds us that we are no longer bond servants but children, no longer slaves but heirs! Our daily work may indeed sometimes look very much like bondage; and there is a sense in which it is: the bondage of the industrial system, of the hopelessly complex economic machine of our day, the bondage of the wage envelope. But this is not the bondage of God. We are not supposed to pretend to enjoy these conditions in themselves; we may even be called upon to try to change them, for ourselves or for others. But, insofar as we are here and now, by sheer necessity, involved in them, subject to them, we have to try to find in them a manifestation of God's will. We must love God's will even through these things, trying to give ourselves to the conditions of our daily work with charity, patience, and faith, knowing that God works in ways mysterious to us.

So, at the beginning of any new work, and of every work-day, let us pray first for an increase in the grace of divine charity, that great motive of love of God moving us in *all* we do—and without which, St. Paul reminds us, all that we do is nothing. Let us try to learn to give that loving service which divine charity makes us capable of, instead of the unwilling drudgery of slaves of this world. And let us pray, too, for the grace of obedience and humility. Even in the imperfect conditions of ordinary employment, there are in fact many aspects of legitimate authority to which we owe obedience in justice, and many circumstances which are occasions of humility. Although Christian humility does not mean spinelessness and there are certainly times when we are bound to speak up for the right, still it is largely through obedience and humility that we offer the oblation of ourselves to God's service.

Then we must ask, too, for the great virtue of fortitude. Fortitude has two characteristics to it. First, it enables us to embark on arduous projects; but secondly—and this is where we need it most—it enables us to sustain the constant strain of recurring minor trials. How much we need it in the monotony, the pettiness, the weariness, of our daily work! And what about virtues like generosity, magnanimity, cheerfulness?

We often become downcast and discontented, not so much by the direct burden of our own work, but because we feel that other people are getting away with less, that it is all being left to us. No peace lies in that direction. We are not answerable for other people's response to grace, but only for our own wholehearted response to the divine call. "Let us not be discouraged then, over our acts of charity; we shall reap when the time comes, if we persevere in them," St. Paul reminds us, and goes on, "Let us work for the good of all, while the opportunity is ours, and above all for those who are one family with us in the faith."

There are other things that might be recalled about our work: the opportunities it brings for spreading the kingdom of Christ, whether it is by our words, our attitude, our example; the occasions to sanctify it more consciously by a prayer, for surely even the most unlikely job must sometimes allow a moment of interior prayer; and, if or when things are at their lowest, the recognition that work is one of the great penitential opportunities of this life. But I think we have already recalled enough to realize that, when we make our morning offering, we can truly consecrate all our long working hours to God, that they too are redeemed and sanctified by Christ, and that through them we can offer loving service to our heavenly Father.

46 | The Mystery of Faith

It is important for us to listen to the experts and to try to understand what they are saying; otherwise, we may remain very dull indeed. But, at the same time, there is a sound instinct which leads us to defend ourselves against the experts —and not only because they often seem to contradict one another. Experience, common sense, right feeling, call it what you will, is also a most important guide. And the more profoundly human the matter is, the more important these deep instincts are. Take, for instance, the life of purity, of kindness, of honesty, of goodness. In one rather horrible way, none of these makes much sense by purely scientific, philosophic, rationalistic standards; yet everything that is best and truest in our humanity is convinced of the value of such a life. We know this; we do not need theoretic proof. There is an element in man which science, metaphysics, argument, cannot really reach, though they can point toward it. This is clearest of all in the deepest thing of all, our life of faith. And we can rightly take comfort in times of crisis about faith, because just as we really know, with all that is best and deepest in us, the truth and value of a life of purity, generosity, gentleness, forgiveness, beyond all the attacks of ridicule or hostility, so, even more, mankind has always turned to God with unshakable hope and love in the life of faith. It is our knowing and loving and communicating with our Creator, with the personal God of us all. It is a most blessed gift: "It is not flesh and blood, it is my Father in heaven that has revealed this to you."

This is not just speculation about abstractions; it is encounter; it is accepting and giving; it is communication at the deepest levels of our personal being with that divine person in whose likeness we are made. Now, in so many ways, the proper fulfillment of our human life and personality comes through communication, through sharing, knowing, understanding, through giving not just our possessions but ourselves. Yet, together with this, paradoxically, it is part of the dignity of our human personality and the price of our personal individuality that there is a final element of incommunicability. A person is unique; a person cannot be divided or absorbed into something or someone else. So, in some deep ultimate sense, persons remain always partly a mystery. How often we discover, even with our nearest and dearest, that we do not really understand them fully, cannot really communicate perfectly. And even God our Creator respects the reality of our personality, of our human dignity and freedom. He does indeed know us, as we can never know ourselves; he loves and dwells in us; he unites us to himself, imperfectly in this world and in some unimaginably blessed happy way in heaven; yet he never destroys our unique personality, that unique self which he himself created us to be.

Encountering so much mystery in each other, in merely finite creaturely persons, it is surely not strange that we should encounter mystery also in the divine person. Indeed, by our own natural philosophy we could only come to know, with difficulty and uncertainty, about God's existence; we could know that he is, but never what he is in his personal life and nature. Yet he himself, we humbly believe, has wanted us to know more than this; his love of us has led him to enable us to know him personally. For love always desires to manifest itself, to reveal its secrets to friends. And so God has made revelation, has invited us to know him by faith. The story of our Christian faith is not really the history of human theology, but the story of divine revelation. It is not really science, philosophy, speculation, though all these must accompany it and help us to grow in understanding. Essentially it is the gift of God's grace, the communication of his own knowledge of himself, Father, Son, and Holy Spirit, given to us through Christ the mediator.

Recent Christian thinking has emphasized faith as our meeting with the living Christ, present and active now, not merely belief in historical record but in present events, in sacramental signs and living encounter. The Church has re-defined herself, not in institutional legal terms, but as the mystery of the people of God, as the personal Christ present and active in living human persons. We do not live by imper-sonal law; our Christian life is not founded on a system of ethics or even on the moral teaching of Jesus. Our life em-braces that teaching, but that is not its essence. We are finally saved by faith in the incarnation, death, and resurrection of Christ. We are saved by our incorporation in Christ, not just in his teaching. It is not joining a Church; it is entering into divine life. Christ is the mediator, the bond of life between God and man. In the Incarnation divine life did not limit itself to the humanity of Jesus; but in him and through him it is communicated to all of us, though in a different manner.

So it is our personal belonging to the personal God through Christ by faith, of which baptism is the effective sign, which gives us life and salvation. Our living by the law is our loving witness to our faith, to our imitation of Christ whose word we believe and whose revelation of the Father's will we love and obey. This is to live by Christ's Spirit, in the freedom of the children of God. For this is not just bondage to a law outside us, but loving service of the Spirit within us. This does not mean, of course, that we do not need external teaching and authority. We joyfully accept God's right to choose the manner of his revelation: "You, therefore, must go out, making disciples of all nations, baptizing them in the name of the Father, and of the Son, and of the Holy Spirit, teaching them to observe all the commandments which I have given you." Our personal acceptance of Christ necessarily takes form and reality by our visible incorporation in the manifestation of salvation history which is the Church. For our faith to bear good fruit it must be engrafted in the good tree, in the living Christ, through all the effective signs which he himself has ordained in his Church.

When St. Peter was given the vision of the transfiguring glory of Christ, he cried, "Lord, it is good for us to be here," that is, to witness the living glory of Christ in visible physical presence. But in fact it was to be otherwise. Our Lord was to insist that it was better for them that he should go, for unless through his saving death he left them, he could not send his life-giving Spirit in power, in universality, in divine freedom and communication. There is in our own time the new challenge of the closeness and immediacy of the whole world, with our universal awareness of all its poor and hungry and desperate, in body and mind and soul. The very scale of the task almost blinds us to its reality. We are tempted by a kind of complacent mentality which sees religion as a very private matter, as not entering uncomfortably into public affairs. There is an immediate outcry to keep religion out of politics when someone gets troublesome about peace, about civil rights, about living conditions. Yet how can our faith manifest any relevance to contemporary man if it ignores these tremendous human responsibilities? We must not forget that divine grace continues to come to us now, not visibly or physically, but spiritually, through the signs of faith. It comes in the power of the Spirit, in the universality of divine love. And today our own faith, our own Church, have to take on this new universality, this new form of witness in their mission.

Assumption

47 | To Hear the Word of God and Keep It

The Assumption of our Blessed Lady, long held in Christian belief, has been formally defined as a part of our faith only in our own time. Although the Assumption is not exactly a key doctrine of our faith, but rather a beautiful flower of it, nevertheless it has always seemed to me that the Assumption is "the answer" to so many of our doubts and fears, a bright light thrown upon our darkness. It is almost as though almighty God said to his ever-questioning children on earth, with all their why's and wherefore's and how long's: "Stop your talk and see; *here's* what it's about, *here's* the end of it all, *here's* what happens when my love is allowed to fulfill its plan." For the assumption of our Lady into heaven is one glorious answer to the apparent futilities and failures of our life on earth. Most of the time our sanctification has to be worked out in a sort of obscurity, through faith, by unlikely means, and without seeing the exact end. But when we contemplate our Lady's assumption, we are granted a glimpse, brief but sufficient, of God's whole plan truly fulfilled in a most wonderful human example.

It is worthwhile to spend some time thinking carefully about our attitude to our Blessed Lady, because true devotion to her is not just an arbitrary decoration of our Catholic religion; true devotion to her is integral to Christian life. But what is this true devotion? It is, first of all, the imitation of her life of faith and love and sacrifice, her utter commitment to the will of God. And, secondly, it is deep confidence in the power of her intercession to help us to achieve this goal. True devotion is not just honoring the glory of the Immaculate Conception, the Virginal Motherhood of God, the Assumption. For what was Mary's supreme and truest glory? Our Lord himself described it when he replied to the enthusiastic woman in the crowd, "Blessed rather are those who hear the word of God and keep it." This was precisely our Lady's own true blessedness, her fullness of grace in the life of faith and love: hearing the word of God and keeping it. That is why generation after generation has called her blessed, recognizing as her own cousin Elizabeth did, "Blessed is she who believed." Blessed, because she had said in faith and love, "Behold the handmaid of the Lord, be it done according to your word."

The Church has always recognized that this is the true and essential glory of Mary. St. Leo said unforgettably, "She conceived him first in her mind before she conceived him in her body"; and St. Augustine declared that she was more blessed in receiving the faith of Christ than in conceiving the flesh of Christ. And the wonderful thing is that it is precisely where she was loveliest, precisely in her true glory, that she is imitable. Her immaculate conception, her virgin motherhood, her assumption, are unique and inimitable; they are the special graces and beauties with which God adorned her for her own personal vocation. But, above all these and more essential than these, was her true holiness, which was to know God by faith and do his holy will; and this is her message to us.

She is given to us as an example in a twofold sense: first, as model of a perfect human response to God's will, and secondly, in a slightly different sense, as a most inspiring and hopeful example of the work of God's grace in our humanity. In this sense her unique privilege of immaculate conception means that in her is seen the perfect fulfillment of the divine concept, the unspoiled work of God's grace in man. And it is that same sanctifying grace which is, by God's mercy, to fulfill itself in each one of us. Not for us in the first moment of our existence; that was hers alone. But even if for us the way be through sorrow and repentance, what does it matter so long as his grace finally prevails and fulfills its work of holiness in us? This is the will of God, our sanctification. And this is why we pray each day, with our Lady and her Son, "Thy will be done."

By the Holy Spirit, by the grace of faith, by the conception of the Redeemer, Mary conceived salvation for us all. She is now the mother of all the redeemed. And her assumption does not make her distant from us; on the contrary, by her special closeness to God and his redemptive love for us, she is made very near to us. Her special place in God's plan for our redemption has become clearer in the Church's consciousness as time goes on. In some ways she seems closer to us now, and stands in a more familiar personal relationship, than in the earlier generations of the Church.

In the Second Vatican Council there was much discussion whether the doctrine about our Lady should be issued as a separate document. But the bishops decided that it should be part of the great Dogmatic Constitution on the Church; and surely the rightful place of our Lady is within the redemptive mystical body of Christ, not apart from it. By her example and by her intercession, she teaches and helps us to make our life in the Church, our life of sacrament and sacrifice, a personal reality in spirit and in truth. The sacraments and all the acts of religion, including the Blessed Eucharist itself,

must be signs of faith and love. Our Lady's total commitment
in faith and loving obedience to the Father's will, in union
with her Son, is given to us for our model and our hope. Our
Lady walked the paths of human life in this world, the same
paths that we find difficult and sometimes apparently pur-
poseless. But she followed them always with one goal, to seek
and fulfill the holy will of God: "Be it done unto me according to your word." In one wonderful sense that response of
hers was made in the name of all mankind, and bears fruit in
her Son's redemptive work until the end of time. Yet each
one of us is called to make truly our own that saving response, in faith and hope and love. We have to try to echo
her *fiat*, whether it be to echo the joy of the Annunciation or
the sorrow of Calvary.

In this way we may turn to our Lady in every circumstance
of our life, for she is never far from us. Nobody in the kingdom of God lives for himself alone, least of all Mary our
Mother. We may most confidently count on her maternal
intercession for us as she prays that we may follow her Son
through the mystery of his life, death, and resurrection. True
devotion to our Lady is a vital, and indeed a most consoling,
part of our Christian faith. The actual form which our "de-
votions" may take will rightly vary according to our personal
temperament, and taste, and grace. But when we dedicate
ourselves or our parishes or our monasteries or our nation to
Mary, we are really only acknowledging that we wish to be
what, in fact, we truly are. For in her Son and in his Church
and in the bond of divine grace we are already bound to her
in the communion of saints. "Pray for us, O holy Mother of
God, that we may be worthy of the promises of Christ. And
after this our exile show unto us the blessed fruit of your
womb, Jesus."

The Kingdom

48 | The True Triumphalism

Two great feasts near the end of the year, the Kingship of Christ and All Saints, both suggest the triumph of Christ and of his followers. But one of the epithets which many Catholics are backing nervously away from in these days of reform and renewal is that of "triumphalism." Now, triumphalism, as I understand it, means that kind of mentality which might be partly expressed in the phrase "God's in his heaven, all's right with the Church." It is indeed humiliating that the ever-present tendency in mankind to be spoiled by good things is found even when it is a question of the good things of God. God has indeed established a good thing upon the earth, his Church, the body of his Son, to continue his redemptive mission. And he has endowed it with divine gifts, with truth and holiness and peace, indeed with the very Spirit of Christ himself. But he did not in fact include among the Beatitudes: "Blessed are you Catholics, for you have it made." Yet we must confess, I think, that sometimes we have managed to give this impression to the world.

We are indeed "a chosen race, a royal priesthood, a consecrated nation," but not chosen to enjoy already the triumph of the kingdom, but rather its missionary labor. We are chosen to follow Christ crucified, to be servants not greater than their Master, who came to minister, to save the world, and who founded his Church to continue his work: to save, to

219

sanctify, to minister. He did indeed endow her with great power for this work, the divine power and divine authority needed for a divine work; and he established in her a divine order, an indispensable apostolic hierarchy. But it was always an authority and power ordained for service, for ministry; hence the truest as well as the most beautiful title of the Vicar of Christ has always been *Servus Servorum Dei*. And every now and again the Church (and this is not exclusively a failing of the hierarchy) has to be reminded of her true vocation, of her true character. She is not called to be an autocratic, complacent body, enjoying here on earth her authority, her security, her law. She is to be a serving Church, a pilgrim Church, following her Lord who was meek and humble of heart, who gave his life for the world.

This means a good deal more than all the prelates taking off their pectoral crosses and jeweled rings, though this might be a striking gesture. There must be a deep realization of what our Christian vocation means, a true conversion of heart, a humble sorrow for failure, a reaching out to men in sincerest love and zeal. This is what lay behind the great gestures of Pope John and Pope Paul which have so reawakened hope and faith in the world and so stirred the hearts of all mankind.

On the feast of All Saints the Gospel reading chosen to proclaim the constitution of Christ's kingdom, and the character of its citizens, tells us: "Blessed are the poor in spirit . . . the patient . . . those who mourn . . . those who hunger and thirst after holiness . . . the merciful . . . the clean of heart . . . the peacemakers . . . those who suffer persecution . . ." Not much place for triumphalism in all that! And, on the feast of the Kingship of Christ, we hear Christ proclaim: "My kingdom is not of this world . . . what I was born for, what I came into the world for, is to bear witness of the truth. Whoever belongs to the truth, listens to my voice."

So two things are very clear. First, the Church of Christ is called to bear witness to the Lord in truth and charity, in patient hope and holy joy. And secondly, we are always in danger of spoiling our ministry by a spirit of pride, of false zeal and bitterness. The treasure is carried in earthen vessels! The sad thing is that there is really such wonderful cause for true joy, for grateful thanksgiving, for boundless hope, for the *right* kind of "triumph." For Christ *has* triumphed over sin; he *has* won his great redemptive victory on the cross. And we are indeed called to share his triumph and his victory, but in his way, his heavenly way, not in our way, our worldly way. We are to triumph over sin, not over sinners; and our victory must be gained by sharing his cross, his loving sacrifice, not by some questionable power play. If only we can keep our attitude right, there need be no limit to the joy, the peace, the hope, the triumph in our Christian life.

The Church triumphant in heaven is really so close to the pilgrim Church on earth; it penetrates it like light, like fire, like life; for both live by the same divine life. There, it is in perfect fulfillment; here, we have beginnings; but they are the wonderful beginnings of eternity. And the feast of All Saints ought to bring us a special realization of this oneness in the kingdom of God. Our senses and our imagination may be cloaked by the mysterious curtain of mortality that enfolds us here, but it is not really an impenetrable curtain; we pass beyond it by our faith, our prayer, our hope, our love. The same love that is in the saints is in us, for it is God's own creative love that courses through all. Our great vocation is to share the work of restoring all things in Christ, so that God may be all in all. That is the holy triumph for which we long.

49 | What Does He Do?

This seems to be an age of achievement—or, rather, of obsession about achievement, which is not the same thing. When people inquire about somebody now, they do not ask, "Who is he?," but "What does he do?" The danger of the older approach was that of snobbishness, with too much emphasis on family and "name"; the danger of the present-day approach may be that we don't care what kind of a person he is, in himself, but what he does. Does he make a lot of money; what is his profession; is he famous, or even notorious, in some way?

Perhaps the better question to ask would be neither who is he, nor what does he do, but *what is he?* Not his family background, nor his visible achievements in the ordinary worldly sense, but what he is in himself. What kind of a person is he? That is what makes us important and successful in the only true way. God loves us not for what we do but for what we are. But we are all children of our own time, and we have to recognize that we are influenced by the attitude of today's world toward "achievements." So we find ourselves not only being impressed by the standards and activities of men and women of the world, but even worried and depressed because of our own "failure." What have we done? We are not famous; we have not made a great career; we have no "specialty." We seem to have our work cut out just to live from day to day.

Achievement and success in this world, while not necessarily opposed to holiness, have in practice very little to do with it. Needless to say, there *ought* to have been a perfect harmony in every aspect of God's creation, in goodness, beauty, peace, achievement of every kind; but now, in man's world, where sin has entered to bring such grievous disorder, the kingdom of God tends to be mainly an interior one. It is still a kingdom of truth and life, of holiness and grace, of justice, love, and peace; but it often finds itself in painful conflict with the kingdom of this world.

The character of the citizens of Christ's kingdom is described in the Sermon on the Mount: "the poor in spirit . . . the patient . . . the merciful . . . the clean of heart . . . the peacemakers . . . those who suffer persecution in the cause of right . . ." Here was the proclamation of the constitution of Christ's kingdom. It was in many ways revolutionary, and its first hearers must have been stunned by the idea that poverty rather than riches, meekness rather than power, patience and suffering rather than success, are marks of the kingdom of God on earth. And notice that our Lord said that these things are marks of the blessed life now, not simply blessed will you be, but blessed are you now. It is not good only because of the reward to come; it *is* good now. The life of grace, the life of the kingdom, is the life of mercy, of poverty, of purity, of patience, of suffering, of peace; this is eternal life, already begun, even though not yet perfectly enjoyed.

This paradoxical state of the child of God on earth was wholly shared by the incarnate Son of God himself. He emptied himself, that he might share everything with us. He, the glory of the Father, the eternal Word, has known what it is to be a man; he has experienced the conditions of this fallen nature of ours, in all its limitations and weaknesses and

pains; he has known what it is to suffer from the follies, the
politics, the injustice, and the contempt of the world. And
since he was a man, it is now forever a happy and worthy
thing to be a man, in spite of all those indignities.

But the great thing is not only that he shared our lowliness, but that he shared with us his divinity. He shared with
us all the heritage that he brought with him to our earth: his
love of his Father, his divine life and holiness, his Holy
Spirit. His communication of all this to us, in our faith and
baptism and grace, makes us infinitely more than mere men.
It gives us the "newness of life" which is a whole new way of
being. It elevates and transforms our life in such a way that
the worldly details and achievements of our ordinary life become quite accidental.

Thus the question "What does he do?" is not very important. The same was asked contemptuously of the Son of God,
Redeemer of the world: "Is not that the carpenter's son? . . .
Can any good come out of Nazareth?" When you are tempted
to discouragement and weariness by the apparent wretched-
ness of ordinary everyday life, think of the thirty years at
Nazareth. The public life of Jesus had its hours of drama
even in the eyes of the world, although it was to end, as it
seemed, in tragic failure. But in the hidden life of Jesus were
years of obscurity and humble monotonous labor, of the
lowly tradesman's dealings with customers, of small-town talk.
What more could the eternal Word do to consecrate our
world and our lot, to walk our paths with us, to comfort and
reassure us? Yet, by the interior oblation of his heart to his
Father, he redeemed and sanctified our humanity so perfectly
that he could say, on the cross, "It is accomplished."

One last point about that other question, "What is he?"
Or, rather, in personal terms, "What am I?" The real answer

lies not in what we *think* we are; that is probably vanity and delusion. Nor does it lie in what, in our moments of truth, we recognize in ourselves as a mixture of rather horrible fraud and pathetic farce. No, the real answer lies in what, by supernatural faith, we believe and know we are: children of God, most dear brethren and members of Christ, citizens of the kingdom of heaven. This is *what* we really are; and this is *who* we really are, the person he knows by name; and this is what we really *do,* by the true talents he gives us, the talents of faith, hope, and charity. "And this is my prayer for you; may your love grow richer and richer yet, in the fullness of its knowledge and the depth of its perception, so that you may learn to prize what is of value."

50 | Beyond All Our Hopes and Dreams

Deep instincts of our humanity, as well as all the tradition of our Christian faith, move us to remembrance and loving prayer for all those who have gone before us through the mystery of death. We speak of them as "the holy souls," and this seems much more fitting than the term used more frequently by our grandparents, "the poor souls." For the great truth is that they have ended their journey through this valley of ours which is still shadowed by sin, and they have entered into God's own eternal kingdom. And that kingdom is above all a place of holiness. If we may single out one of the attributes of God to try to describe him most truly, though of course none of them can adequately compass his infinite being, it must be the attribute of holiness. Holy, holy, holy Lord God of hosts—this is the eternal proclamation of heaven. And the first vital grace which God communicates to those whom he has called to himself is holiness. Before all the other gifts of heavenly life which we love to enumerate, peace and joy and light and the rest, he must first give us holiness; for without this we are separated from him, and while we are separated from him, there can be no peace nor joy nor light.

Perhaps we are inclined to think that this is precisely the problem. We may fancy that somehow we can imagine ourselves sharing divine peace and joy, but it is much harder to imagine ourselves (and perhaps, to be honest, some of our acquaintances) sharing divine holiness. Well, first of all, this is by no means an unsound instinct. It is good to have a humble consciousness of our sinfulness, to be aware that so much in us is contrary to holiness, and to realize that our truest and most needed prayer is "Lord, be merciful to me a sinner."

But then we must go on to remember that this is precisely the divine work which is to be done in us; this, our sanctification, is the will of God. This is really the greatest of his wonders: his truly miraculous transformation of his creatures, making them children of light, children of his holiness. This is his supreme gift to us, something that only he can do: "He has given us great promises, by which we are made partakers in the divine nature." No words, even these bold words of St. Peter, can ever really describe the truly divine work which God himself brings about in us, a work only conceivable through the gift of faith, a faith itself made possible only because it believes in God's infinite love and, therefore, in his infinitely loving deeds.

But the gifts of God always reflect the truth and the reality of God and of his acts. His operation in us is true and real, and it is given according to the truth and reality of the human nature in which he himself created us. When he calls us holy, children of God, members of his kingdom, these gifts are true gifts; they really are *ours* now. They are not some external legal fiction, some "assignment of title," something from outside the receiver. They are interior, made in keeping with our human nature. God, and God alone, as Creator of our nature, can thus work in us from within. He acts by his enabling grace so that our own mind and will truly share in his action, truly accept and will his gift, truly respond to his creative power. God never destroys or falsifies; he always bestows reality, being, truth.

And, most of all, his supreme work of sanctification in us is to be a *true* work; we are to be made *truly* holy. How is this possible? We cannot really understand this mystery of his infinite goodness to us. We can only say it is true holiness because it is from him; and it is truly ours because it is given by his true creative gift. This great work is to be completed in us, either on this earth, as we see so wonderfully achieved in those souls we call saints, or else in that mysterious state we call purgatory. There, it seems, all the power and ardor of God's sanctifying grace, which somehow in our willfulness we manage partly to elude on earth, is at last concentrated like fire upon the soul. It is really something glorious, and at last wholly desired and consented to. At the same time, however, this direct encounter of our imperfection with the burning holiness of God is also a piercing anguish to our conscience. The word of God is like a fiery sword, reaching to the very division between soul and spirit, quick to distinguish every thought and design in our hearts.

So the Christian instinct has rightly always been to intercede for the holy souls, to pray for their release from sin. It is not that we intercede for them for some kind of shortcut through purgatory, some kind of exemption from its purifying fire. We pray, rather, that the divine work may indeed be completed; we pray that they may be released, not so much from purgatory, but from all trace of sin, from everything that is not holy, not divine. And this is precisely the wonderful height of Christian hope and faith—namely, that finally God's work *will* be completed in us, that we shall be truly holy, truly as he intended us to be, truly without any trace of sin. How is this possible? Only because of the *creative* power in all his actions: when God forgives, he forgives creatively. There is not just a negative character about his action, as there may be in ours when we try to forgive. We try to pretend that nothing has happened; we try to forget. But his pardon is much more than that; it is positive, restorative, life-giving, making holy. There is a beautiful prayer in the missal which begins "God the restorer and lover of INNOCENCE . . ." The word "innocence" means much more than sin forgotten, much more than an attempt to forget and start again. Or, if it is to start again, it is to do so in a truly divine sense, a new creation, a new life, not an old one patched up. By divine pardon sin is "wiped out" (an expression scripture itself uses), obliterated from the soul; and holiness, innocence, is divinely communicated to the soul from the source of all holiness, God's own holy being.

This is the divine purpose; and although man's willfulness has brought sin and suffering into creation, yet God's holy purpose will be fulfilled in the end. The feast of the Immaculate Conception of our Lady reminds us again of a sublime example of the holiness which God's grace brings about in a creature when nothing impedes its effect. Mary begins full of grace, sinless; and her greatest title is "Holy Mary." But that same grace is intended by God to bring about its effects in us, too. In our case this will be fulfilled, not by sinlessness from the beginning, but by repentance and pardon; but the end will be the same: true holiness. For there will be nothing but holiness in heaven. Humbly but peacefully, we rest all our hope in the holy will of God, which is our sanctification. For "he whose power is at work in us is powerful enough, and more than powerful enough, to carry out his purpose beyond all our hopes and dreams."

The Ending
of the Year

51 | Light and Darkness, Bless the Lord

A special characteristic of the spirit of the Church at the end of the year is the virtue of hope. It is one of the clearest qualities of our prayer, both in the closing weeks of the time after Pentecost and in the new beginnings of Advent. As the old year ends, there are all those great glimpses of the triumphant plan of divine love, as exemplified in the feasts of the Kingship of Christ, All Saints, and All Souls. Then too, our hope finds strength and peace in the contemplation of the holy will of God, as emphasized in the liturgy of the Sunday Masses. There is, one always feels, a special "homing" spirit in the Church toward the end of the year. In the Epistle of the Twenty-third Sunday after Pentecost, St. Paul warns of those whose minds are set on the things of earth, "whereas we find our true home in heaven. It is to heaven that we look expectantly for the coming of our Lord Jesus Christ to save us." And the Introit for the same Sunday promises the peace of God: "I will listen when you cry to me, and bring the scattered exiles home."

And hope is so wonderfully renewed, enlivened, deepened, as Advent begins for us again the whole story of the Incarnation and the Redemption. As we prepare for the birth of our Savior, we are already enlightened and warmed by the first rays of the sun of justice arising upon us once more: "All my heart goes out to you; my God, I trust in you . . ." And as we receive already in sacramental communion the divine pledge of love and salvation in the body and blood of our Lord, we sing of the transforming consecration which the birth of Christ will bring to our humanity: "The Lord will give goodness, and our earth shall yield her fruit." Sometimes the miseries and sins of ourselves and of the world press heavily upon us; but how can we ever lose hope when we remember the blessed fruit that our earth has yielded in the incarnation of the Son of God?

Certainly our hope is refreshed and confirmed by these bright glimpses of the divine horizon. It is good, and necessary, that our eyes should be raised sometimes, above the dark valleys of this life, to the eternal hills. Without these moments when we are in a special way "alive to God," glimpsing the divine wisdom "reaching from end to end, strongly and sweetly ordering all things," we should become too wearied and discouraged in the narrow paths of time. But let us remind ourselves, very clearly again, that these moments of light are not the essence of hope itself. Hope plays its real part in the darkness, not in the light, not so much when we enjoy a glimpse of the goal as when the vision is past and we have to drop our gaze again to the immediate surroundings on our way to the goal. And hope is at its greatest and purest when things seem at their darkest, when, as we say, we "hope against hope," that is, when we are without any sense of security through understanding or knowledge or consolation, but are casting our trust purely and wholly in the loving power of God alone.

In the catechism we learned that hope is a supernatural gift of God by which we firmly trust that he will give us eternal life and all the means necessary to obtain it. It is perhaps that part about "the means necessary" which is the key, and the difficulty, of the virtue of hope. It is not too hard to have a rather vague hope that somehow God will bring us to heaven in the end. The practical difficulty is rather to recognize and trust God in the means he gives us to attain that end, to live in hope, in a spirit of trust in God's providence and love, finding and accepting in the realities around us the means of our sanctification, the means to fulfill the whole wonder of our divine vocation. The temptation always is to expect *other* means, ones we would have preferred ourselves; and while we complain and wait for these, we fail to recognize and use the means God's wisdom has in fact chosen for us.

In some ways, hope and resignation would seem quite different things: hope leading us still to expect the best, resignation helping us to accept the worst, so to speak. But they are not really so opposed. If by resignation we accept something that is a sorrow and disappointment for us, we are really doing so because we still hope and trust, in spite of this mysterious development, that God's plan, though not ours, will still work out—for his glory and our true good.

Perhaps these words of St. Paul, in the Epistle for the Last Sunday after Pentecost, may help us to understand a little better this great question of the knowledge of God's will: "Brethren, we have been praying for you, unceasingly. Our prayer is, that you may be filled with that closer knowledge of God's will which brings all wisdom and all spiritual insight with it." We know that the only final and essential petition of all prayer is that we may rightly know and do God's will. But there are various ways in which the knowledge of God's will may grow in us. There are, first of all, the true and wonderful ways which we call "enlightenment," or spiritual understanding. These ways help, in a rather clear and positive and intelligible manner, to build up the supernatural

wisdom and character of a man. With these there is no need
of explanation or justification: they bring light, peace, and
love; our only duty is to accept them thankfully when they
come.

But there are other ways in which the knowledge of God's
will does need some explaining, because it is a knowledge
which may not look or feel much like what we ordinarily
mean by knowledge. Knowledge usually suggests to us
things like security, clarity, confidence; and these qualities
are not always felt in the action of God's will in us. Perhaps
St. Paul is including this other kind of knowledge when he
says a little further on in the same Epistle: "May you be
inspired as his glorious power can inspire you, with full
strength to be patient and to endure." Are not patience and
endurance qualities more usually associated with mystery
than with knowledge, with darkness rather than with light?

Thus we are reminded that although we are to thank God
for making us fit to share the light which saints inherit, for
rescuing us from the power of darkness and transferring us to
the kingdom of his beloved Son, yet, even with all this wonder of our divine vocation, it remains true that at times,
parodoxically, we share in the light of saints in a manner
which often keeps *us* in the dark, in a manner which calls for
us to be patient and to endure.

It is very familiar to us, this spiritual doctrine which tells
us that much of the time God will be working in us, and we
shall be seeking him, through our darkness, through trust,
faith, humility, patience. But the fact is that this lesson is
never finally learned and done with; although we know the
general theory of it, each concrete case touching ourselves
tends to be a new little crisis for us, and it always will be.

Why is this? Well, we know that the essential condition of

true spiritual life is a total giving of ourselves to God's will. Let us hope that we are trying to be as sincere as we can when we call this the real purpose of our life. The trouble is, however, we think we know the program ahead of us; consequently, we are always getting confused, disappointed, unsettled, at the way things in fact work out. For one thing, we do not find the changes we hoped for. There is so much sameness in ourselves and in our difficulties; there is no recognizable progress, sometimes even no recognizable direction; there is no comforting assurance that we are really getting anywhere, no sense of security, no real feeling that we are now once and for all given to God and that now all is safely in *his* care. So we are tempted to take things in our own hands again, to try to make them work out "right," *our* way.

Yet, is not all this precisely the point? Is not all this absolutely necessary if our surrender, our abandonment to God's will, is really to be complete? It is our acceptance of all these things, without really understanding them, without really recognizing the divine hand at work, that *is* the real surrender. If we had the satisfaction of perceiving the exact character and purposes of the sacrifice, then obviously much of its value would be lost. A man must really lose his life to find it; the seed must truly die if it is to bear fruit.

Of course, we are much too weak for this to be going on all the time. Mostly God leads us as we are able, giving us a little light, a little consolation, a little peace. But at times the purifying and deepening occasions of grace will be offered to us also: the moments of darkness, as well as the moments of light. These are perhaps the really crucial steps toward that purity of heart which is the great aim of the Christian life.

"Out of the depths I have cried to you, O Lord . . ." I suppose we often use such a prayer at times when the so-

called "depths" of our troubles are really very shallow indeed
and we are simply making a good deal of splash. Well, that is
all right; but most of all, surely, this great psalm is a prayer
for the heart *really* in darkness, really feeling the depths of
failure, loneliness, insecurity, yet still turning to God in the
darkness, turning for the strength to be patient and to endure, "as befits his servants, waiting continually on his
pleasure."

Lord, if you will have me in light, blessed be your name;
If you will have me in darkness, blessed be your name;
Light and darkness, bless the Lord.